Unmasking Control: A Guide to Beneficial Ownership Transparency

Editors
Richard Berkhout
Francisca Fernando

Cataloging-in-Publication Data
IMF Library

Names: Berkhout, Richard, editor. | Fernando, Francisca, editor. | International
     Monetary Fund, publisher.
Title: Unmasking control : a guide to beneficial ownership transparency /
     Editors Richard Berkhout, Francisca Fernando.
Other titles: A guide to beneficial ownership transparency
Description: Washington, DC : International Monetary Fund, 2022. | Includes
     bibliographical references and index.
Identifiers: ISBN 9798400208041 (paper)
Subjects: LCSH: Persons (Law). | Money laundering – Law and legislation.
Classification: LCC K625 .B47 2022

DISCLAIMER: The views expressed in this book are those of the
authors and do not necessarily represent the views of the IMF's
Executive Directors, its management, or any of its members. The
boundaries, colors, denominations, and any other information
shown on the maps do not imply, on the part of the International
Monetary Fund, any judgment on the legal status of any territory
or any endorsement or acceptance of such boundaries. All information presented herein is accurate as of press date.

Recommended citation: Berkhout, Richard, and Fernando, Francisca, eds. 2022.
     Unmasking Control: A Guide to Beneficial Ownership Transparency.
     Washington, DC: International Monetary Fund.

ISBN: 9798400208041 (paper)
     9798400208140 (ePub)
     9798400208188 (PDF)

Please send orders to:

International Monetary Fund, Publication Services
P.O. Box 92780, Washington, D.C. 20090, U.S.A.
Tel.: (202) 623–7430 Fax: (202) 623–7201
E-mail: publications@imf.org
Internet: www.elibrary.imf.org
www.bookstore.imf.org

Contents

Foreword

The IMF has been concerned for some time with the lack of transparency of companies' and other types of legal persons' beneficial ownership information. Not knowing the identity of the beneficial owners—that is, the persons who own and control legal persons—allows criminals to misuse these entities to hide their identities and the criminal origins of their assets, and to enjoy the proceeds of crimes. This negatively affects countries' economies.

Revelations from data leaks such as the 2016 Panama Papers, the 2017 Paradise Papers, and the 2021 Pandora Papers have spotlighted the abuse of legal persons for money laundering and terrorist financing purposes. They also raised awareness of the importance of beneficial ownership transparency, an issue now at the forefront of the international agenda.

The IMF's Executive Board has endorsed the Financial Action Task Force's (FATF) international standards for anti–money laundering and combating the financing of terrorism, which include beneficial ownership requirements (as part of the FATF's 40 Recommendations). These standards were issued in the early 2000s, and much guidance has been provided on this topic over the years, but implementing beneficial ownership requirements effectively is still a challenge for many countries. The FATF recently enhanced its beneficial ownership requirements in March 2022.

This issue is particularly relevant to the IMF because countries that fail to implement these measures effectively can expose themselves and other countries to money laundering, terrorist financing, and other inherent risks and may be unable to protect the integrity of their financial systems. This exposes countries to broader macroeconomic risks, and it is in countries' economic interest to take steps to enhance the transparency of beneficial ownership information.

Clearly, beneficial ownership information not only is important for the overall effectiveness of countries' frameworks for anti–money laundering and combating the financing of terrorism, but also supports other important policy agendas and initiatives. For example, countries can use beneficial ownership information to improve the business environment, ensuring that legal persons are not misused to avoid tax responsibilities. Access to beneficial ownership information can support anti-corruption efforts (preventing public officials from hiding illicit wealth) and limit opportunities for abuse in awarding public procurement or extractive contracts. A comprehensive system for holding beneficial ownership information can support national security initiatives, for example, by ensuring that designated persons do not continue to operate under a new name, even in the territory of the sanctioning state.

Therefore, the IMF is keen to continue assisting its membership in enhancing the transparency of beneficial ownership information available within countries. IMF staff have been increasingly addressing these issues in the context of IMF surveillance, lending, and capacity building. To support our ongoing work in this area, the IMF's Legal Department wrote this guide to assist countries in effectively implementing the FATF international standards for anti–money laundering and combating the financing of terrorism. The guide also aims to strengthen our members' economies and mitigate the inherent risks resulting from a lack of beneficial ownership transparency by building on the recent revisions to the standards to enhance the transparency of legal persons. We hope it will be a useful tool for countries planning to implement comprehensive systems for holding adequate, accurate, and up-to-date beneficial ownership information.

Bo Li
Deputy Managing Director
International Monetary Fund

Acknowledgments

Many people have taken the time to support this work, and to contribute and share their expertise with us. We are very grateful to them.

In particular, we would like to thank Rhoda Weeks-Brown (General Counsel and Director of the IMF's Legal Department) and Yan Liu (IMF Deputy General Counsel) for their support and Nadim Kyriakos-Saad (IMF Assistant General Counsel) for his oversight of this project.

We would also like to extend our special thanks to the members of the IMF Legal Department's Financial Integrity Group Transparency of Beneficial Ownership Working Group for all their contributions to this project: Adrian Wardzynski, Grace Jackson, Heena Gupta, Indulekha Thomas, Ivana Rossi, Santiago Texido Mora, and Robin Sykes contributed their expertise on relevant issues, reviewed several iterations of this book, and conducted research to support its drafting.

This project also benefited from the insightful comments of Tanna Chong (Financial Action Task Force Secretariat), Maira Martini (Transparency International), Tymon Kiepe (Open Ownership), Thom Townsend (Open Ownership), Lindsey Marchessault (Open Contracting Partnership), and Andres Knobel (Tax Justice Network).

Several current and former colleagues also supported this project through review and contributions during different stages of development, including Arz Murr, Elizabeth Ebeka, Brendan Crowley, Christophe Waerzeggers, Cecilia Marian, Chady El Khoury, Emmanuel Mathias, Eric Robert, Jay Purcell, Jane Duasing, Kohei Noda, Kathleen Kao, Ke Chen, Marjorie Henriquez, Nadine Schwarz, Steve Dawe, and Yara Esquivel Soto.

We would also like to gratefully acknowledge the support of Rafaela Calomeni and Rosemary Fielden, who provided excellent administrative support; the IMF Legal Department's Resource and Information Management Unit for their budgetary support; and the IMF's Communications Department, and in particular Lorraine Coffey, for their work in managing all the aspects of production of this book.

Finally, none of this would have been possible without the support of the donors to Phase II and III of the IMF's AML/CFT Thematic Fund who funded this important project: Canada, France, Germany, Japan, Korea, Luxembourg, the Netherlands, Norway, Qatar, Saudi Arabia, Switzerland, and the United Kingdom.

Preface

Identifying who ultimately owns or controls companies and other types of corporate structures (the beneficial owner) is a key financial integrity measure that also has important governance and transparency objectives and is relevant for macroeconomic and financial stability. Improved beneficial ownership transparency helps countries better understand on whose behalf money is moved and assets are owned, which in turn helps these countries to tackle illicit financial flows and prevent the laundering of proceeds of crime, including corruption.

The IMF's Legal Department has long recognized the relevance of this issue and is actively working to provide advice to our member countries in enhancing their frameworks for beneficial ownership information. We have raised these issues in the IMF's annual surveillance discussions with its member countries in cases where lack of transparency of companies is considered to have macro-critical impact in a country, and have supported including structural reforms related to beneficial ownership transparency in select IMF lending programs. In the context of our pandemic-related emergency financing, we called for countries to commit to publish beneficial ownership of companies awarded public procurement contracts, and we are providing technical assistance and training to help countries implement beneficial ownership transparency. We have also worked with the Financial Action Task Force—the international standard setter for anti–money laundering and combating the financing of terrorism—to update beneficial ownership requirements, most recently in March 2022.

This book is a guide for practitioners, other relevant stakeholders, and interested parties to support their efforts in establishing comprehensive frameworks for holding beneficial ownership information. We will also use it to further our own work in this area, including providing more targeted technical assistance and training on this topic.

I am grateful to the donors of the AML/CFT Thematic Trust Fund for their generous contribution to this project, all the external reviewers and contributors who shared their experiences with us, and the outstanding staff of the Legal Department, who continue to make important contributions on these important issues.

Rhoda Weeks-Brown
General Counsel and Director
Legal Department
International Monetary Fund

Editors and Contributors

Editors

Richard Berkhout is a deputy unit chief with the Financial Integrity Group of the IMF's Legal Department where he is overseeing anti-money laundering, combating the financing of terrorism (AML/CFT), and other illicit finance topics in relation to all IMF workstreams. Before joining the IMF, he was a senior policy analyst at the Financial Action Task Force (FATF) Secretariat, responsible for FATF's mutual evaluation program, standard setting, and leading assessments. Before that, he was with the Ministry of Finance of the Netherlands as a senior policy advisor at the Financial Markets Directorate. He holds a Master's degree in law and political science from the University of Leiden in the Netherlands.

Francisca Fernando is a counsel with the Financial Integrity Group of the IMF's Legal Department, working on AML/CFT and financial integrity–related issues in the context of IMF technical assistance, surveillance, lending, and policy work. Before joining the IMF, she worked in the Financial Market Integrity Unit of the World Bank Group and for the Stolen Asset Recovery Initiative of the World Bank Group and the United Nations Office of Drugs and Crime. She holds a Master of Laws from the University of Toronto, a Bachelor of Laws from the London School of Economics and Political Science, and is called to the Bar of England and Wales.

Contributors

Alexander Malden is a research officer with the Financial Integrity Group of the IMF's Legal Department. Before joining the IMF, he worked as a governance officer at the Natural Resource Governance Institute. Before that, he was a policy consultant at S&P Global Market Intelligence. He earned a Master of Science from the University College London School of Public Policy and a Bachelor of Arts in international relations from Queen Mary, University of London.

Ian Matthews is a lawyer and consultant specializing in the financial services, supervisory, and beneficial ownership aspects of AML/CFT. Previously, he worked at the Financial Conduct Authority in the United Kingdom as a specialist in international AML/CFT matters. He was co-chair of the FATF's Evaluations and Compliance Group, which is responsible for overseeing the conduct of the global mutual evaluation process. He is currently a scientific expert for financial issues for the Council of Europe's MONEYVAL committee.

Jonathan Pampolina is a counsel with the Financial Integrity Group of the IMF's Legal Department. He previously worked at the Supreme Court of the Philippines and the Department of Interior and Local Government, and practiced litigation in a top-tier law firm in Manila. He earned a Master of Laws from Georgetown University (under a Fulbright Scholarship), a Bachelor of Laws from the University of the Philippines, and an undergraduate degree in management from the Ateneo de Manila University.

Lia Umans is a financial sector expert with the IMF's Legal Department and an independent consultant with over 25 years of experience in AML/CFT. From 2008 to 2019, she was a policy analyst at the FATF Secretariat where she made crucial contributions to the global AML/CFT assessment process and the FATF's work on identifying and responding to high-risk and noncooperative jurisdictions. Before that, she held various management positions at the Belgian Financial Intelligence Unit and co-chaired the Training Working Group of the Egmont Group of financial intelligence units. She holds a Master's degree in commercial and financial sciences from the University of Hasselt, Belgium.

Abbreviations and Acronyms

AML/CFT	anti–money laundering and combating the financing of terrorism
BO	beneficial ownership
CDD	customer due diligence
DNFBP	designated nonfinancial businesses and professions
EITI	Extractive Industries Transparency Initiative
FATF	Financial Action Task Force
FI	financial institution
FIU	financial intelligence unit
F&P	fit and proper
Global Forum	Global Forum on Transparency and Exchange of Information for Tax Purposes
LLC	limited liability company
LLP	limited liability partnership
ML	money laundering
OECD	Organisation for Economic Co-operation and Development
PEP	politically exposed person
TCSP	trust and company service provider
TF	terrorist financing
TFS	targeted financial sanctions

Glossary

Accurate: Information (in the context of beneficial ownership information) is considered accurate when it has been verified to confirm its accuracy by checking the identity and status of the beneficial owner using reliable, independently sourced or obtained documents, data, or information.

Adequate: Information (in the context of beneficial ownership information) is considered adequate when it is sufficient to identify the natural person or persons who are the beneficial owner or owners and the means and mechanisms through which they exercise beneficial ownership or control.

Alternative mechanism: An alternative mechanism (in the context of the collection of beneficial ownership information) is another mechanism or form—other than information held by a public authority or body—that allows adequate, accurate, and up-to-date beneficial ownership information to be obtained, held, and accessed in a timely and efficient manner.

Basic information: This is the minimum information that the international standards for anti–money laundering and combating the financing of terrorism (AML/CFT) require about a legal person, including—but not limited to—its legal ownership, control structure, shareholders, and directors. This information should be publicly available through a company registry.

Bearer shares and bearer share warrants: These are negotiable instruments that transfer ownership or entitlement to ownership in a legal person to the person who holds the physical bearer share or bearer share warrant certificate and any other similar instruments or warrants without traceability.

Beneficial owner: This is the natural person or persons who ultimately own or control a customer and it also refers to the natural person on whose behalf a transaction is conducted. It also includes those natural persons who exercise ultimate effective control over a legal person or arrangement.

Beneficial ownership information: This is the information collected to identify the beneficial owner of a legal person. Beneficial ownership information should be adequate, accurate, and up to date.

Company registry: This is a register of companies incorporated or licensed in a country and normally maintained by or for the incorporating authority. This register typically holds basic information (see definition of "basic information").

Competent authorities: Competent authorities in this context are considered public authorities with designated responsibilities for combating money laundering, terrorist financing, or proliferation financing. These can include—but are not limited to—a country's financial intelligence unit; institutions responsible for investigating and prosecuting money laundering and its associated underlying crimes, terrorist financing, and proliferation financing; and authorities that have AML/CFT supervisory or monitoring responsibilities.

Customer due diligence: This is the process for collecting and evaluating information about legal or natural persons to identify and assess and mitigate the risk of conducting a business relationship with them.

Designated nonfinancial businesses and professions (DNFBPs): Designated categories of nonfinancial businesses and professions in this context are entities other than financial institutions that have AML/CFT obligations. These include—but are not limited to—casinos, real estate agents, dealers in precious metals and stones, lawyers, notaries and other types of legal professionals and accountants, and trust and company service providers. Gatekeepers can often be DNFBPs (see definition of "gatekeepers").

Financial Action Task Force (FATF): The FATF is an intergovernmental body whose purpose is to set standards and promote effective implementation of legal, regulatory, and operational measures for combating money laundering, terrorist financing, and proliferation financing.

FATF Recommendations (the international AML/CFT standards): The FATF developed a series of recommendations recognized as the international standards for combating money laundering, terrorist financing, and proliferation financing.

Gatekeepers: This is often used as a general, colloquial term for financial institutions and DNFBPs. In this guide, this broadly refers to a subset of DNFBPs—including lawyers, notaries, and accountants; trust and company service providers; and in some instances, financial institutions—that offers legal and financial services with respect to the creation, incorporation, and registration and provision of services for legal persons.

Law enforcement authorities: These are authorities responsible for enforcing a country's laws, such as the police services.

Legal arrangement: These are types of legal constructs such as express trusts or other similar legal arrangements, including depending on the country context, some types of *fiducie, treuhand, waqf,* and *fideicomiso.*

Legal person: The FATF defines legal person as any entity other than a natural person that can establish a permanent customer relationship with a financial institution or otherwise own property.

Natural person: A natural person is a human being and is distinguished from a legal person.

Nominator: The nominator refers to an individual (or group of individuals) or legal person that issues instructions (directly or indirectly) to a nominee to act on their behalf in the capacity of a director or a shareholder, also sometimes referred to as a shadow director or silent partner.

Nominee, nominee director, or nominee shareholder: These terms refer to an individual or legal person instructed by another individual or legal person (the nominator) to act on their behalf in a certain capacity regarding a legal person. This can include a nominee director (also known as a resident director) who is an individual or legal entity that routinely exercises the functions of the director in the company on behalf of and subject to the direct or indirect instructions of the nominator. It can also include a nominee shareholder who exercises the associated voting rights according to the instructions of the nominator and/or receives dividends on behalf of the nominator.

Registry: A registry (in the context of this guide) is defined broadly as a mechanism/database that holds information on a legal person. This can include multiple databases if they are interlinked, consistent, and offer centralized access to information. A registry can also be public.

Supervisors: FATF defines supervisors as "designated competent authorities or nonpublic bodies with responsibilities aimed at ensuring compliance by financial institutions and/or DNFBPs with requirements to combat money laundering and terrorist financing."

Timely access: This is the ability to source relevant information rapidly and efficiently. Access to timely information by competent authorities is important, especially in the context of ongoing investigations or monitoring by competent authorities. For effectiveness, this requires that the information should already be directly accessible.

Up to date: This is information that is as current as possible and is updated within a reasonable period (for example, within one month) after any changes.

Note: Several terms of the key terminology are sourced from FATF (n.d.-a) and FATF (n.d.-b).

CHAPTER 1

Introduction

Countries' efforts to fight criminal activity—including money laundering and terrorist financing—are often obstructed because of the challenges of finding out who truly owns and controls, and benefits from, the legal entities (such as companies and other types of corporate vehicles) used in the context of these illicit activities. Most countries have systems for obtaining information on legal ownership (that is, the person or legal entity who is the legal titleholder), but the legal owner is not necessarily who ultimately owns and controls the entity. There is a need to go one step further to identify the beneficial owner (that is, the real human being who owns and controls the legal entity). Many countries have inadequate systems or no system at all for holding information on these beneficial owners.

The concept of beneficial ownership of a legal person is different from legal ownership. Legal ownership is often defined by shareholdings or membership and can include ownership by other legal persons (for example, a legal person can be a shareholder in another legal person). Beneficial ownership information relates to information about the natural person who ultimately owns or controls a legal person, including when ownership is established through a chain of ownership or by means other than direct control (for example, a natural person who can direct a legal person's affairs and decision making but who does not necessarily own any part of the legal person). Beneficial ownership information will not always be apparent on the face of documentation maintained by or on behalf of a legal person.

Ensuring timely access to adequate, accurate, and up-to-date beneficial ownership information of legal persons is important for countries to mitigate the misuse of legal persons in criminal activities. Chapter 2 explains some of the common vulnerabilities and threats associated with the misuse of different types of legal persons.

In March 2022, the Financial Action Task Force—an intergovernmental body that sets the international standards for anti–money laundering and combating the financing of terrorism through its 40 Recommendations—adopted changes to the standards concerning requirements for collecting and holding beneficial ownership information and ensuring that relevant authorities can have timely access (FATF 2012).This guide aims to explain these requirements (focusing on how countries can achieve these objectives effectively) by considering the IMF staff's ongoing work in this area, including in assisting countries on beneficial ownership transparency issues in the context of IMF surveillance, lending, financial sector assessments, and capacity development work.[1]

---

[1] This is intended to complement the upcoming Financial Action Task Force guidance on Recommendation 24: Transparency and Beneficial Ownership of Legal Persons.

Chapter 3 considers the various sources of beneficial ownership information, including their strengths and limitations, and suggests best practices to ensure that this information is adequate, accurate, and up to date. It also traces when beneficial ownership information should be collected and updated throughout the life cycle of a legal person.

Chapter 4 discusses the importance of beneficial ownership transparency for both the overall effectiveness of countries' frameworks for anti–money laundering and combating the financing of terrorism and for efforts to fight criminal activity (such as tax evasion, corruption, and illicit financial flows) and to improve the business environment. It also discusses strengthening transparency, accountability, and governance (for example, procurement, asset disclosure and declaration frameworks, governance of natural resources) and supporting national security initiatives more generally. It makes the case for why countries should aim to put a comprehensive system in place for holding beneficial ownership information that meets the needs of all these different policy objectives and allows them to reap the benefits of beneficial ownership transparency for their broader economic growth.

Chapter 5 provides policymakers, advisors, and practitioners with guidance on essential elements that they need to consider when reviewing existing systems or deciding on establishing and implementing new systems for obtaining and holding adequate, accurate, and up-to-date information on the beneficial ownership of legal persons.

Along with the discussion, the guide proposes questions to facilitate strategic thinking of these issues among the different stakeholders. These guiding questions are a starting point to support the subsequent decision-making processes. Eventually, a country must choose to implement systems that are specific to its own circumstances. (Guiding questions are included throughout the chapters and as a stand-alone checklist in Appendix 1.)

The aim of the guide is to focus on the overarching principles required to establish an effective system, and thus it intentionally avoids including references to any specific country best practices or models that may have varying degrees of implementation and effectiveness. There is no silver bullet solution, and what works for one country might not work for another. Appendix 4 (Useful Resources) provides a list of current country references as an additional resource.

This guide builds on already existing guidance and other relevant material on beneficial ownership, including those published by the Financial Action Task Force, the World Bank, the Global Forum on Transparency and Exchange of Information for Tax Purposes, and relevant civil society organizations working in this area. The exclusive focus is on beneficial ownership issues of legal persons (companies and other types of legal entities), and it does not extend to the identification of beneficial owners of legal arrangements (for example, trusts) except for when they are part of the ownership chain of a legal person.

REFERENCES

Financial Action Task Force (FATF). 2012. *International Standards on Combating Money Laundering and the Financing of Terrorism and Proliferation: The FATF Recommendations,* updated March 2022. Paris: Financial Action Task Force. https://www.fatf-gafi.org/media/fatf /documents/recommendations/pdfs/FATF%20Recommendations%202012.pdf.

CHAPTER 2

Key Concepts Related to Transparency of Legal Persons

Beneficial ownership always refers to a natural person, never a legal person or a legal arrangement. Although complex and confusing structures create myriad opportunities for a beneficial owner to hide their control of legal persons or to conceal the transfer of assets, countries can count on key concepts to navigate the maze.

BENEFICIAL OWNERSHIP AND THE INTERNATIONAL STANDARDS

The Financial Action Task Force's (FATF) international standards for anti–money laundering and combating the financing of terrorism (AML/CFT) define the concept of beneficial ownership. A beneficial owner is:

> The natural person(s) who ultimately owns or controls a customer and/or the natural person on whose behalf a transaction is being conducted. It also includes those natural persons who exercise ultimate effective control over a legal person or arrangement. Only a natural person can be an ultimate beneficial owner, and more than one natural person can be the ultimate beneficial owner of a given legal entity or arrangement.

The beneficial owner is always a real human being, commonly referred to as the "natural person." It can never be the "legal person" or "legal arrangement," which are legal constructs based on a law (for example, a company or a trust). The expressions "ultimately owns or controls" and "ultimate effective control" refer to situations in which ownership and/or control is exercised through a chain of ownership or through control other than direct control. This definition makes it clear that a beneficial owner can never be a legal person or a legal arrangement, even if legal entities may own or control other legal persons, especially when there is a chain of ownership. The terms "beneficial owner" and "ultimate beneficial owner" are often used synonymously, but "beneficial owner" is intended to refer to the natural person or persons who ultimately own or control a customer, and/or the natural persons on whose behalf a transaction is being conducted. Accordingly, the two terms have the same meaning.

The FATF Standards

The FATF AML/CFT international standards set out requirements to enhance the transparency of legal persons, including regarding the availability of adequate, accurate, and up-to-date beneficial ownership information. These measures are important to help prevent the misuse of legal persons.

International standards are one of the drivers for countries to implement systems to ensure beneficial owner transparency. The best-known standards are the FATF's 40 Recommendations, which the IMF's Executive Board has endorsed. The FATF's mandate is to set standards and promote effective implementation of legal, regulatory, and operational measures for combating money laundering, terrorist financing, proliferation financing, and other related threats to the international financial system's integrity (FATF 2012, Introduction).

The FATF requirements for measures to ensure transparency of beneficial ownership information have been in place since 2003 and were updated in 2012. In March 2022, the FATF adopted enhanced requirements relating to the transparency of legal persons, which are set out in FATF Recommendation 24 and its Interpretive Note. The FATF is concerned with the effective implementation of its recommendations (which is measured based on 11 immediate outcomes, of which Immediate Outcome 5 is concerned with the transparency of legal persons), but in general, countries have faced considerable challenges with effectively implementing the international standards for beneficial ownership transparency.[1] The text of Recommendation 24 and Immediate Outcome 5 is set out in Box 2.1.

The aim of Immediate Outcome 5 and the enhanced requirements for Recommendation 24 is to prevent the misuse of legal persons and to ensure access to beneficial ownership information for competent authorities. At its core, Recommendation 24 is a requirement for authorities to obtain and hold this information when legal persons are created. To do this, the technical compliance standard places various requirements on countries, including to put a legal framework in place to ensure that basic and beneficial ownership is captured accurately, that basic information is publicly available, and that beneficial ownership information is available to competent authorities. The requirements apply at one or more of the

---

[1] As of February 2022, 120 of the 205 countries and jurisdictions that are part of FATF's global network have been assessed against the 2012 FATF recommendations. Regarding beneficial ownership transparency, none was considered compliant with Recommendation 24, and only 37 were found largely compliant. Sixty-five countries were partially compliant and 18 countries noncompliant. Regarding the prevention of legal persons and arrangements for money laundering and terrorist financing purposes, and the availability of their beneficial ownership to competent authorities (Immediate Outcome 5), no country reached a high level of effectiveness, 11 reached a substantial level, 53 reached a moderate level, and 56 reached a low level. For an updated analysis, see the FATF Report on State of Effectiveness and Compliance with the FATF Standard (FATF 2022).

creation, registration, and/or incorporation stages of the legal person and remain relevant during its lifetime and even at and after dissolution (see Box 2.1).

Box 2.1. FATF Core Requirements regarding Transparency of Beneficial Ownership

Immediate Outcome 5

Legal persons and arrangements are prevented from misuse for money laundering or terrorist financing, and information on their beneficial ownership is available to competent authorities without impediments.

Characteristics of an effective system

Measures are in place to:

- Prevent legal persons and arrangements from being used for criminal purposes;
- Make legal persons and arrangements sufficiently transparent; and
- Ensure that accurate and up-to-date basic and beneficial ownership information is available on a timely basis.

Basic information is available publicly, and beneficial ownership information is available to competent authorities. Persons who breach these measures are subject to effective, proportionate, and dissuasive sanctions. This results in legal persons and arrangements being unattractive for criminals to misuse for money laundering and terrorist financing.

Recommendation 24: Transparency and Beneficial Ownership of Legal Persons

Countries should assess the risks of misuse of legal persons for money laundering or terrorist financing, and take measures to prevent their misuse. Countries should ensure that there is adequate, accurate and up-to-date information on the beneficial ownership and control of legal persons that can be obtained or accessed rapidly and efficiently by competent authorities, through either a register of beneficial ownership or an alternative mechanism. Countries should not permit legal persons to issue new bearer shares or bearer share warrants, and take measures to prevent the misuse of existing bearer shares and bearer share warrants. Countries should take effective measures to ensure that nominee shareholders and directors are not misused for money laundering or terrorist financing. Countries should consider facilitating access to beneficial ownership and control information by financial institutions and DNFBPs undertaking the requirements set out in Recommendations 10 and 22.

Source: FATF Standards and FATF Methodology.

Note: A copy of the most recent changes proposed to FATF Recommendation 24 is included in Appendix 2 and shown in Figure 2.1.

Transparency of beneficial ownership requirements are also relevant for Recommendation 25, which concerns the transparency of trusts and other types of legal arrangements. The requirements are also relevant for several other FATF recommendations, including regarding understanding risks, customer due diligence (CDD), politically exposed persons, wire transfers, fit and proper tests for ownership of financial institutions, and international cooperation. It is particularly important for CDD requirements because these feed into the requirements of Recommendation 24 (as an information source) but also rely on beneficial ownership information that is available pursuant to this recommendation. As a result, shortcomings in the implementation of Recommendation 24 can have a negative impact on other FATF recommendations.

Immediate Outcome 5 assesses the extent to which countries have put effective measures in place to prevent legal persons and arrangements from being used for criminal purposes, make legal persons and arrangements sufficiently transparent, and ensure that accurate and up-to-date basic and beneficial ownership information is available on a timely basis. As with technical compliance, lack of effectiveness in the implementation of beneficial ownership requirements can affect immediate outcomes beyond Immediate Outcome 5, and it is relevant (though less directly) to all the other 10 immediate outcomes (see Appendix 3).

Figure 2.1 illustrates how the different elements of Recommendation 24 interact with each other.

Other Standard Setters and Initiatives on Beneficial Ownership

Other standard-setting bodies have also incorporated requirements related to beneficial ownership. This includes the Global Forum on Transparency and Exchange of Information for Tax Purposes (Global Forum), which is the international arrangement for monitoring and conducting peer reviews on the implementation of the international standards on transparency and exchange of information for tax purposes (that is, the Exchange of Information on Request Standard and the Automatic Exchange of Financial Account Information Standard). The concept of beneficial ownership, as defined under the FATF recommendations, features prominently under these two tax standards because knowing the identity of the natural persons behind entities helps preserve the tax systems' integrity and enables tax jurisdictions to achieve their tax goals. In addition, the United Nations Convention against Corruption reiterates the need for countries to implement beneficial ownership identification as part of the measures to prevent money laundering stemming from proceeds of corruption (Article 14) and to take reasonable steps to determine the identity of beneficial owners of funds deposited into high-value accounts, both to prevent and detect the transfers of proceeds of crime (Article 52) (UNODC 2003). The concept of beneficial owner is not elaborated, but an indication of who may be considered a beneficial owner is included in the technical guide to the United Nations Convention against Corruption (UNODC 2009).[2]

Beneficial ownership requirements also feature in industry and other private sector standards. The Extractive Industries Transparency Initiative Standards

---

[2] The technical guide to the United Nations Convention against Corruption suggests that the term "beneficial owner" should be regarded as covering any person with a direct or indirect interest in or control over assets or transactions, along with varying requirements for identification and verification.

Figure 2.1. Requirements under FATF Recommendation 24

Legal Person
(For example, company)

Basic Information

Beneficial Ownership (BO) Information

In public **company registry**

Maintained by **company** at registered office or **location** notified to company registry

Obtained and maintained by **company**

Company name; proof of incorporation; legal form and status; address of registered office; basic regulating powers; list of directors; unique identifiers (if applicable)

Location of register of shareholders (if applicable)

Nominee status, identity of nominator (where applicable)

Register of shareholders or members, names, number of shares held, and categories of shares of shareholders (including nature of voting rights)

Public Authority/Body: such as FIU, tax authority, company registry, BO registry; interconnected registries **Or Alternative Mechanism**

Also hold information on nominee status, identity of nominator (where applicable); identifying information

Supplementary measures: Information held by regulators or stock exchange (for listed companies) or obtained by FIs and DNFBPs

Available to Competent Authorities (Particularly Law Enforcement Authorities and FIUs)
Cooperation by companies, FIs and DNFBPs
Powers for competent authorities to access information
Access to basic and BO information in the course of public procurement

Exchange information on shareholders

Necessary for international cooperation

Monitor quality of assistance

Facilitate access by foreign authorities to basic information

BO information should be available to foreign authorities

Obtain BO information on behalf of foreign counterparts; avoid unduly restrictive conditions on exchange of information or assistance; designate and make publicly known the agency(ies) responsible for responding to international requests

(Continued)

Figure 2.1. Continued

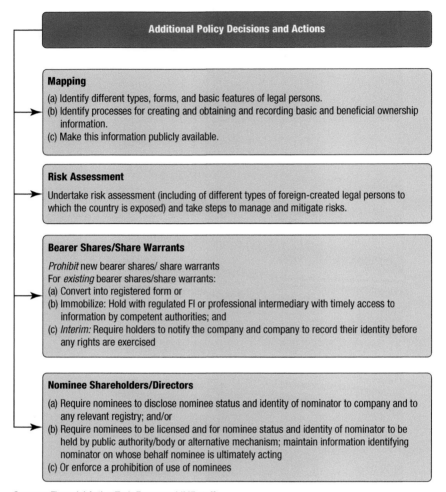

Additional Policy Decisions and Actions

Mapping
(a) Identify different types, forms, and basic features of legal persons.
(b) Identify processes for creating and obtaining and recording basic and beneficial ownership information.
(c) Make this information publicly available.

Risk Assessment
Undertake risk assessment (including of different types of foreign-created legal persons to which the country is exposed) and take steps to manage and mitigate risks.

Bearer Shares/Share Warrants
Prohibit new bearer shares/ share warrants
For *existing* bearer shares/share warrants:
(a) Convert into registered form or
(b) Immobilize: Hold with regulated FI or professional intermediary with timely access to information by competent authorities; and
(c) *Interim:* Require holders to notify the company and company to record their identity before any rights are exercised

Nominee Shareholders/Directors
(a) Require nominees to disclose nominee status and identity of nominator to company and to any relevant registry; and/or
(b) Require nominees to be licensed and for nominee status and identity of nominator to be held by public authority/body or alternative mechanism; maintain information identifying nominator on whose behalf nominee is ultimately acting
(c) Or enforce a prohibition of use of nominees

Sources: Financial Action Task Force; and IMF staff.
Note: BO = beneficial ownership; DNFBP = designated nonfinancial businesses and professions; FI = financial institution; FIU = financial intelligence unit.

promote good governance of oil, gas, and mineral resources. One of the requirements of this standard (Requirement 2.5) is to recommend publicly available beneficial ownership registers for corporate entities that apply for or hold an interest in the relevant industries (EITI 2019, 18). The Wolfsberg Group, which is an association of 13 global banks, develops frameworks and guidance for the management of financial crime risks for banks. Its 2012 anti–money laundering principles for private banking include requirements related to beneficial ownership and its implementation (Wolfsberg Group 2012b).

Other supranational and regional initiatives and high-level political commitments have helped promote transparency of beneficial ownership. For example, the European Union has been taking steps to implement the relevant FATF requirements through legislation, including by requiring its member countries to implement public registries of beneficial ownership information. At the Group of Twenty meeting in Sydney, Australia, in 2014, member countries agreed to high-level principles on beneficial ownership. Among others, these principles urge countries to ensure that beneficial ownership information is kept in the country, and is adequate, accurate, and current (Principle 3) (G20 2014, 2).

These initiatives reinforce the relevance of beneficial ownership issues to other policy agendas (see Chapter 4). However, in some instances, they may also fall short of the FATF approach to beneficial ownership, and in such cases, countries should focus on following the FATF's definition of beneficial ownership.[3] More broadly, countries should aim to put a holistic and comprehensive system in place for collecting and maintaining beneficial ownership information in a country that can support these different objectives instead of adopting a piecemeal approach to different initiatives, which may have varying requirements.

TYPES OF LEGAL PERSONS

> *Even if the names of different categories of legal persons are the same between jurisdictions (for example, limited liability companies, limited liability partnerships, partnerships, and foundations), their characteristics and use in practice can vary significantly between jurisdictions.*

Most (if not all) countries have developed legal frameworks that regulate the creation of legal persons. In general, these frameworks attribute a series of legal rights and obligations to legal persons, including the right to own movable and immovable property and to enter into contracts, thereby enabling them to play an essential role in commercial and entrepreneurial activity.

The types of legal persons that can be set up in a specific country are unique to the country's legal and regulatory framework. Even if they are known by similar names or titles in individual countries, they are likely to have different characteristics and different legal requirements.

Mapping of Legal Persons

In line with FATF standards, countries are required to have mechanisms that identify and describe the different types, forms, and basic features of legal persons in the

---

[3] For example, because of their narrow sectoral focus, compliance with the Extractive Industries Transparency Initiative (EITI) standards alone will not satisfy the FATF requirements that apply to all companies, whereas compliance with the FATF requirements would have a positive impact on compliance with the EITI standards.

country. In practice, this means that competent anti–money laundering authorities need to list and keep a comprehensive overview of all existing types and forms of legal persons, including a description of their relevant features (see Box 2.2). In addition, those authorities should describe the processes for creating each of those types of legal persons and for obtaining and recording both basic and beneficial ownership information. This includes being aware of all the relevant laws and regulations establishing the legal persons (which is also relevant for technical compliance). The FATF standards require that this information on types of legal persons and processes is publicly available. It is important that these authorities know the legal persons that can be created and/or operate in their jurisdictions so that they have an idea of how natural persons might use these entities and from which entities they need to collect information. To understand a country's systems from an AML/CFT perspective, it is necessary to centralize and organize this information for the purposes of the AML/CFT risk assessment (see "Risk Assessments of Legal Persons").

When mapping the information, countries should focus not only on the primary law that regulates most of the basic features of most legal persons in a country (for example, company law, civil code) but also consider other relevant laws (including supranational legislation) that may allow for the creation of specialized legal persons (for example, legal persons that carry out special functions, such as asset protection) and laws that change the features of legal persons (such as the ability to change jurisdiction of residence) or afford them special treatment (such as special tax status). In general, no one type of legal person, a priori, should be excluded from this mapping exercise just because at first sight, they might give the impression that they are not particularly relevant for AML/CFT purposes (for example, associations, state-owned enterprises, and statutory corporations whose governance arrangements are usually embedded in their governing laws).[4]

At the outset, it is important to remember that although legal persons might have the same name in different countries or even the same origin in a common legal framework, their specific features might nevertheless differ between countries because of evolving differences in the legal frameworks governing the establishment and functioning of legal persons. In addition, vulnerabilities of specific types of legal persons are also likely to be different between countries, considering the money laundering and terrorist financing risks and context that individual countries present. This has consequences for discussions with counterparts in other jurisdictions (for example, for mutual legal assistance requests or as part of an assessment), and it is important to keep in mind that the simple name of a legal person, especially when translated to another language, is of limited value on its own in determining its characteristics and risks.

---

[4] The specific levels of ownership, control, and functions required for an entity to be considered a state-owned enterprise differ on a country-by-country basis. Given this, it can often be difficult to establish which entities are state owned and conversely whether a state-owned enterprise has privately owned shares. The inclusion of state-owned enterprises in the mapping of legal persons can help inform an assessment as to whether a state-owned enterprise should be subject to beneficial ownership disclosure requirements.

The FATF standards do not describe a specific process for the mapping exercise, nor do they impose any rules for putting the overview of legal persons together. Countries have flexibility in deciding on the format if they ensure that all types of legal persons that can be set up in the country are duly reflected. Countries can choose a general description of the various categories of legal persons accompanied by the specific features for each of these categories.

It is possible to describe some broad categories of legal persons that are present in countries. The following list is by no means meant to be an extensive overview of all types of legal entities and their features in different legal systems.

- *Companies.* One of the most widely used legal structures is frequently referred to as a company or corporation. In some countries, companies or corporations are mentioned in the domestic legal framework as specific and distinct types of legal persons, but in other countries, the term "company" or "corporation" is just a nonlegal generic term used to designate *any* legal person that undertakes commercial activity for profit. Even the FATF mixes the terms "legal persons" and "company" in different parts of the standards. The term "companies" can also extend to legal persons whose main object is not strictly commercial, such as holding companies, which are often created to buy and hold the shares of other companies.[5] Either way, the term "companies" often refers to the legal persons that are the primary tool for serving as the main vehicles for corporate commercial activities.

  Companies are usually characterized by precise ownership interests that may carry different rights and liabilities and the separate legal personality of the company itself. In addition, there is a clear distinction between the ownership (shareholders) and the management/control of the company (board of directors). Companies also tend to be incorporated under a statutory regime versus some other types of legal person (for example, associations) that can be established by agreement. Typically, natural and legal persons invest in a company through ownership of shares in the company, and shares can be owned by natural persons, legal persons, and legal arrangements. There are different categories of shareholders, notably those that have voting rights and those that do not. Voting shareholders elect the board of directors to run the company and vote on key decisions relating to the company's activities.

  Companies (that is, company shares) can generally be (i) publicly traded on the stock exchange (public companies and corporations), (ii) owned by the state, (iii) private companies (with varying restrictions), or (iv) variations of those three.[6] Many countries also recognize the concept of limited liabil-

---

[5] In addition, some countries have statutory corporations, which, though practice varies from country to country, often have no shareholders and are set up and governed by legislation. Examples include state broadcasting authorities and railways.

[6] For an extensive analysis of the characteristics of a corporation, see Armour, Hansmann, and Kraakman (2009, 6–15).

ity companies,[7] which are a hybrid between companies and partnerships, whereby ownership and control rights are determined by contract and are dependent on the amount of capital contribution by the investors.

- *Partnerships.* Such entities are usually established between two or more partners (being natural and/or legal persons) to conduct business activities. In some countries, partnerships do not have a separate legal existence independent of their members or partners. In its simplest form, all partners are jointly liable for any debts and obligations pertaining to the business (general partnerships). In other instances, some of the partners may relinquish management of the business activities in exchange for limited personal liability. These may also be called limited partnerships, limited liability partnerships (which are a hybrid between companies and partnerships), or such ones called *société en commandite*.

- *Foundations.* These can be used to own property or other assets for a specific and explicitly stated purpose (such as charitable purposes or for tax reasons). Such entities are usually managed by a board of directors that is responsible for the foundation's operations.[8] Nonprofit organizations and charities are often incorporated as foundations. That said, in some jurisdictions, foundations may be allowed to engage in for-profit activities or be a tax planning vehicle (OECD 2001, 27).

- *Associations, cooperatives, and mutual societies.* These are legal persons formed by a group of people (members) who enter into an agreement to achieve a common objective or purpose. These persons can be formed for commercial or noncommercial purposes—including of a religious, social, or educational nature—and may fully independently engage in activities and transactions to achieve their stipulated objectives in their own names, without having to identify the individual members that make up the association, cooperative, or mutual society.

  Cooperatives are typically set up to achieve a shared common goal, including for commercial purposes. Their ownership can be shared among a group of people, such as workers (worker cooperatives) or users (consumer cooperatives), or by several other legal persons. Cooperative businesses can be

---

[7] Examples of limited liability companies in different countries include limited liability company (LLC) in the United States; private limited company (Pvt. Ltd.) in Hong Kong Special Administrative Region, India, Ireland, and the United Kingdom; Gesellschaft mit beschränkter Haftung (GmbH) in Austria, Germany, and Lichtenstein; besloten vennootschap (BV) in the Netherlands; and société à responsabilité limitée (SARL) in France (FATF Risk, Trends, and Methods Group report).

[8] According to the definition developed by the European Foundation Center (http://www.efc.be/), Charitable "Foundations are separately constituted nonprofit bodies with their own established and reliable source of income (usually, but not exclusively) from an endowment or capital. These bodies have their own governing board. They distribute their financial resources for educational, cultural, religious, social, or other public benefit purposes either by supporting associations, charities, educational institutions, or individuals or by operating their own programs." See also O'Halloran (2012, 196–201) on the lack of an agreed system for mutual recognition of foundations in Europe.

profit making, with the profits being shared among members or reused for investment and future growth. They may also conduct financial business on behalf of their members, such as credit unions or building societies.

- *Anstalt.* This type of legal person is typically incorporated in civil law jurisdictions. An anstalt does not consist of members or participants, and it does not have any shareholders, but it is set up by one or more founders who can either be a natural or legal person who maintains control over the anstalt. This type of legal person provides the founders with increased protection of anonymity with only limited disclosure. They can have a commercial or noncommercial purpose but are most often used to park assets for tax planning purposes.

In addition to knowing the companies incorporated under a country's domestic legal framework, the revised FATF standards now require that countries are also aware of the risks of foreign legal persons who present money laundering or terrorist financing risks and have a sufficient link to the country. This will require country authorities to perform some sort of preliminary mapping exercise to understand what types of foreign companies are operating in their country or have another type of link to the country. The FATF has included some examples of what could be a sufficient link on a risk basis. Examples of sufficiency tests may include—but are not limited to—when a company has permanent establishment/branch/agency, has significant business activity, or has significant and ongoing relations with financial institutions or designated nonfinancial businesses and professions (DNFBPs); is subject to AML/CFT regulation; has significant real estate/other local investment; employs staff; or is a tax resident in the country. In conducting mapping exercises, authorities should look beyond their own domestic legal frameworks and have an understanding of the type of legal structures that can be created elsewhere, noting that the names of these legal structures can vary between countries.

Box 2.2. Guiding Questions: Mapping of Legal Persons

Mapping Exercise

- Has the country carried out a mapping exercise that covers *all* legal persons that can be set up in the country or have sufficient links with it?
- Does this exercise capture any relevant recent changes in legislation, processes for the creation of legal persons, processes to ensure that basic and beneficial ownership information is obtained and maintained?
- Does the mapping exercise also cover legal persons having sufficient links in the country but established or created outside the country (for example, domestic registration of foreign legal persons)?
- Have all types of existing governing legislation, enforceable means, and guidance (for example, at federal, state, and supranational levels) been identified and taken into consideration?
- Does the country keep a comprehensive overview of all relevant laws and enforceable means providing the legal framework for legal persons that can be created? Is this overview publicly available? Where?

(Continued)

Box 2.2. Continued

- Does it give a clear indication (for example, through links) of where to find the various laws and enforceable means, relevant articles of these laws and enforceable means, and so on?
- Did competent authorities issue any guidance targeting effective implementation by individuals and professionals creating and managing legal persons to ensure that individual persons and professionals have an adequate understanding of what information should be delivered (by the person initiating the creation of the legal person) or obtained (by the professional involved in the creation and management of the legal person)?

Features of Legal Persons

- Do the various laws and enforceable means clearly set out
  - All types of legal person(s) that can be set up under each of these laws and enforceable means?
  - The basic features of all types of legal persons?
- Is this information publicly available, and can all relevant aspects (for example, type, form, and basic features) be easily identified? Where?
- Are there any other means that the country relies on to assist with the identification of all types, forms, and basic features of legal persons (for example, a summary document by the authorities)?

Processes for Creation

- What is the process to follow for the creation of each type of legal person? (List each type and how it can be set up.)
  - Can this information on process be easily accessed?
  - Is this information publicly available?
- Are requirements on basic and beneficial ownership information clearly set out?
- Is there any relevant guidance for the public (for example, on identification data and documents to be provided)?
  - Where can it be found?

Public Availability of Information

- How is the information setting out the previously mentioned mechanisms, processes, and requirements made available to the public?
  - Is there guidance to the public on how to get access to this information?
  - Is access direct through one or more central/decentralized government websites or other online platforms?
- Is access free of charge? If not, what are the costs associated with this access?

VULNERABILITIES AND THREATS OF LEGAL PERSONS

> *Legal persons can be misused to facilitate criminal acts. As a first step to mitigating these risks, countries should understand the vulnerabilities and threats associated with different types of legal persons that are created/operate in or have a sufficient link to their countries.*

Legal persons are key for the functioning of any economy, but the potential for their misuse is also well documented. This chapter gives a high-level description of some of the vulnerabilities and threats that lead to the misuse of legal persons. For a comprehensive overview of threats and vulnerabilities of legal persons, countries should refer to existing detailed guidance and best practices papers, typologies reports, and other studies issued by several international bodies (see World Bank [2011]; FATF [2006, 2014, 2018, 2019]; and Global Forum and IDB [2019]).

Although the vulnerabilities and methods differ, most (if not all) types of abuse of legal persons aim to hide the natural person that is the ultimate owner or controller of the company. This is because there are requirements on natural persons to identify themselves (for example, if they own bank accounts). The primary way for natural persons to operate anonymously is by owning or controlling legal persons.

Vulnerability Descriptions

Several possible factors may contribute to making a legal person more vulnerable to misuse, depending on the circumstances. Note that some of these factors may arise because of legitimate reasons.

Complex Ownership and Control Structures

In some instances, complex and multitiered ownership and control structures may be used to obscure ownership (for example, control structures that involve many different layers and tiers of ownership or involve several shareholders). Shares in one company can be owned by another legal person or a legal arrangement, which in turn are owned by yet another different legal person, and so on. This makes it more difficult to identify the beneficial owners or controllers at the end of the ownership chain.

In general, one can expect that official representatives of legal persons should understand their ownership and control structure and know the identities of the beneficial owners. The revised FATF standards now expect companies to obtain and hold adequate, accurate, and up-to-date information on the company's own beneficial ownership. They should be able to explain that structure to competent authorities, obliged entities, and those persons with a valid interest in knowing this information. Competent authorities and other third parties could see representatives' lack of ability to understand and/or refusal to explain the ownership or control structure as a red flag and prompt obliged entities to apply enhanced scrutiny measures on relationships and transactions with these legal persons.

Confusing Ownership and Control Structures

Ownership and control over a legal person are two separate concepts, and it should not be assumed that a certain percentage of ownership in a legal person will also mean the same level of control. For instance, complex ownership structures could allow minority shareholders to exercise control over legal persons (including where there are undisclosed agreements between those minority shareholders). The same goal to obscure the control structure can be achieved through issuing shares with voting rights and others without voting rights. As a result, the number of shares needed to control a legal person can easily go below any of the thresholds that countries may use to define beneficial ownership (for example, 25 percent, 20 percent, or 10 percent). This shows that ownership is not the sole determinant of control over a legal person.

Other scenarios can also determine control, such as debt instrument arrangements, in which a lender or creditor can control a legal person via the provisions of the lending agreement or by a third party who can otherwise influence a shareholder by means of a financial or other relationship. This is why the FATF's definition of beneficial ownership separates the concepts of ownership and of control and goes to the extent of referring to those persons who exercise ultimate effective control over a legal person or arrangement.

Complex Multijurisdictional Structures

Complex structures are often multijurisdictional, with a legal person in one country owned or controlled by legal persons in one or more other countries. The chain of ownership may therefore be spread across several jurisdictions, which is likely to create significant impediments when law enforcement authorities are investigating a legal person, including those caused by a lack of timely access to information on beneficial owners. These impediments can also extend to other competent authorities (for example, financial intelligence units, supervisors, tax authorities) and obliged entities when they are interacting with the legal person. This vulnerability can be exacerbated when the country where the legal person was created and registered has low or no transparency requirements or even allows information on beneficial owners to be held in a country other than the country of creation/registration of the legal person (third-party introducers). In addition, distinguishing between ownership and control can be particularly difficult when assessing foreign-created legal persons—their structures may be well understood in the country of origin but not in another jurisdiction.

Ease of Concealing and/or Transferring Ownership

Multiple tools allow for the easy transfer of ownership along with a high degree of anonymity. For example, bearer shares—in their basic, unregulated form—are company shares in certificate form, and whoever is in physical possession of them is considered their owner (just like cash). This allows for complete anonymity in transferring ownership and control. Another tool that continues to exist and can be easily misused to ensure anonymity is the concept of nominee shareholders and directors. Although nominees can be used for legitimate purposes, the fact that a nominee holds shares for the benefit of or acts on behalf of another natural or legal person (whose identity is not disclosed) complicates the identification of the beneficial owners. The revised FATF standards impose additional measures on bearer shares and nominees (see discussion in Chapter 3 of "Bearer Shares and Share Warrants").

In some countries, foreign legal persons can operate or conduct business relationships without having to be reincorporated under the laws of the second jurisdiction, which can further complicate investigations involving such companies. Although the legal person likely remains fully domiciled in the original country of incorporation/formation, the legal person is offering products and/or services to customers or owns assets or conducts operations in a second jurisdiction, and beneficial ownership information might not automatically be available in the second jurisdiction. Competent authorities in the second jurisdiction should have timely access to basic and beneficial ownership information of those foreign legal persons. The revised FATF standards now require that countries take measures to mitigate against the risks of foreign legal persons that present money laundering or terrorist financing risks and have a sufficient link to the country, which can include requirements to hold beneficial ownership information (see the discussion in Chapter 3).

Use of Intermediaries in Forming Legal Persons

Professional intermediaries—including lawyers, notaries, accountants, financial or wealth management advisors, tax advisors, and trust and company service providers—are so-called gatekeepers that are retained for the creation and/or management of legal persons, depending on the jurisdiction. They provide specialist advice for financial, business, tax, and personal matters and can help set up particularly complex ownership and control structures, often to shield assets from various types of liability to which their true owners may become subject or to minimize tax liabilities.

Criminals may also rely on these intermediaries to set up legal persons and act as front persons, nominee shareholders, and directors to facilitate money laundering activities and other crimes.[9] Obtaining information from gatekeepers has proved challenging, especially those that benefit from professional secrecy or claim legal professional privilege, or that operate in jurisdictions where they are

---

[9] See, for example, FATF and Egmont Group (2018, Section 3) and reports and prosecutions stemming from the Panama Papers and Luanda leaks (for example, https://www.justice.gov/opa/pr /us-accountant-panama-papers-investigation-sentenced-prison; and https://www.icij.org/investigations /luanda-leaks/).

not required to hold this information. These challenges are exacerbated when professionals from multiple jurisdictions are involved in the creation of corporate structures. However, it would be incorrect to say that gatekeepers are an impediment to access to information and transparency in all cases. On the contrary, well-regulated gatekeepers with a high level of professional integrity support effective identification and verification of beneficial ownership information.

Legal Arrangements as Part of Control/Ownership Structures

The use of legal arrangements in the control and ownership structure of a legal person can further complicate all the previous examples.[10] Legal arrangements (such as trusts) are very heterogeneous and highly flexible, and they can be set up with or without gatekeepers, based on the legal system of a jurisdiction of choice. Trusts are essentially an agreement among parties, each with a defined role and responsibility (for example, settlor, trustee, beneficiary, and [in some cases] protector) aimed at separating legal ownership and control (that the trustee holds) from the benefit (economic or social that is attributed to the beneficiary or beneficiaries). Often, trusts may not require any registration, do not possess legal personality, and are unknown to the authorities in the country that provided the legal framework for their creation. Trustees usually have only fiduciary obligations to their beneficiaries but may also be unregulated (such as in the case of non-professional trustees) and may not be subject to even rudimentary obligations such as proper record keeping.[11]

The use of legal arrangements to obscure beneficial ownership is most often associated with building additional layers of complexity to hide ownership (FATF and Egmont Group 2018). For example, a legal person might have a legal arrangement as one of its shareholders and vice versa. Given that a legal arrangement might have a different natural person as the legal owner/trustee, the beneficiary, and the controller, then tracing the beneficial owner who exerts control becomes more complicated, especially because many legal arrangements are not registered. In addition, the precise relationship of ownership/control within the legal arrangement itself is likely to be determined by law in the jurisdiction in which the legal arrangement is set up and by the terms of the legal arrangement itself (for example, the trust deed). Even though some countries may not enable trusts and other types of legal arrangements to be formed within their

---

[10] In FATF terms, "legal arrangements" refers to express trusts or other similar legal arrangements, such as *fiducie*, *treuhand*, and *fideicomiso*. Legal arrangements such as trusts separate the legal property, administration, and economic benefit of an asset. As such, the beneficial ownership of property subject to a trust-like legal arrangement might be exercised by one person (for example, the trustee, who has legal ownership of the asset) or be influenced by more than one legal person in circumstances, for example, where the settlor might still be exercising discretion over who benefits from the asset. Some legal arrangements can be created without the need to produce formal documentation to competent authorities, and thus proving the beneficial owner can be difficult.

[11] A review of FATF's Recommendation 25, which covers beneficial ownership transparency of trusts and other types of legal arrangements, is currently ongoing.

jurisdiction, it still does not necessarily prevent foreign legal arrangements from being customers of financial and other institutions in that country.

Threat Descriptions

Criminal actors may take advantage of the vulnerabilities associated with legal persons to facilitate criminal activities. Although much has already been written about the misuse of legal persons, the following are additional resources that set out common examples of misuse:

- *Money laundering and terrorist financing.* The extent to which legal persons have been misused for money laundering and terrorist financing purposes is well known and widely reported, including through FATF typologies, such as FATF (2019).

- *Tax crimes.* Legal persons can also be used to facilitate tax offenses. For more detailed information on the global response to this issue, see Global Forum and IDB (2019).

- *Corruption.* Companies have been used to hide the proceeds of corruption in most large-scale corruption cases. This was highlighted by work undertaken by the World Bank and the United Nations Office on Drugs and Crime's Stolen Asset Recovery Initiative, whose report analyzed 150 cases of grand corruption and determined that companies had been misused in 128 of such cases (Van der Does de Willebois and others 2011).

- *Fraud.* Legal persons can be used to defraud customers—for example, people may invest in or purchase goods and services from companies with no legitimate business activities, only for those companies to disappear without a trace or be found to be shell or straw companies without any assets to compensate victims. The lack of ownership or control information makes it difficult for customers to recover their money from these criminals. For example, see OECD (2021).

- *Trade-based crimes.* Legal persons assume particular relevance in international trade transactions, in which large-scale exporters, importers, shipping companies, and facilitators are inevitably legal persons. In some instances, legal persons may be used to facilitate trade-based money laundering, for example, through instances of collusion between legal persons or the use of shell companies to conduct fraudulent or illicit transactions. Examples of this are elaborated in FATF and Egmont Group (2020).

- *National security risks.* Designated natural and legal persons on sanctions lists can find ways to evade United Nations and other bilateral sanctions by owning assets (for example, real estate) or financing activities through other legal persons (DOJ 2017). Likewise, legal persons have also been used to circumvent prohibitions-related trade bans, and legal persons have been set up and used as de facto banks to facilitate financial transactions to avoid bans (UN 2015, sections VIII and IX). The absence of transparency of beneficial ownership information enables such activities, and countries that fail to prohibit such activities are making themselves vulnerable for (secondary) targeted financial sanctions.

- *Political interferences.* The lack of transparency of legal persons can also give rise to the potential for political interference through indirect means. For example, other countries, parties, or persons who wish to influence the political discourse or decision-making processes to further their self-interests and avoid anti-bribery/corruption legislation can fund political campaigns through front companies or shell companies without having to disclose their identity as beneficial owners of these entities—for example, see Doublet (2011).

- *Disguising ownership and control of financial institutions.* Legal persons can be misused to disguise the true ownership and control of financial institutions, with the aim to distort fit and proper requirements. This can be particularly concerning where criminals gain control of financial institutions and use them to launder proceeds of crime without being detected. The Basel Committee on Banking Supervision (2012) notes that licensing authorities should have the authority to set the criteria for fit and proper assessments, and this is also included in European Central Bank (2021).

RISK ASSESSMENTS OF LEGAL PERSONS

> *Countries should have a comprehensive understanding of how legal persons could be misused in their country—regardless of whether they are domestic or foreign-created legal persons—if they operate in or have a sufficient link to the country.*

Domestic Legal Persons

Given the potential for misuse of legal persons, the FATF standards require countries to assess the money laundering and terrorist financing risks associated with each type of legal person created (that is, incorporated and/or registered) in the country and to take appropriate steps to manage and mitigate these risks. Based on the mapping of legal persons (see Chapter 2, "Mapping of Legal Persons"), this should involve an exercise that considers, among other things, the money laundering and terrorist financing threats and vulnerabilities in the framework relating to legal persons, how legal persons are used for commercial and noncommercial activities within the jurisdiction, and the potential criminal activity that may be perpetrated by using legal persons. This exercise should ultimately inform the country's policies, including whether the appropriate legal structure exists to meet the relevant criteria of the international standards, and the allocation of resources to mitigate the threat of money laundering and terrorist financing.

Although there is no set format for the risk assessment of legal persons, countries may consider undertaking the legal person risk assessment as part of their national money laundering and terrorist financing risk assessment or as a stand-alone risk assessment exercise. The FATF has issued guidance on how to undertake a national risk assessment, and countries can rely on different technical assistance providers (for example, the IMF's national risk assessment tool and the World Bank's national risk assessment tool that includes a module covering shell companies and beneficial ownership–related risks) or the private sector in this regard (FATF 2013). In conducting a risk assessment of legal persons, countries should consult widely, including to get inputs from obliged persons (that have legal persons as their customers) and independent experts from academia and civil society looking at issues related to the transparency of legal persons (see Chapter 4, "Other Applications for Beneficial Ownership Information").

At a minimum, the risk assessment of legal persons can consider the following information:

- The number of each (sub)type of legal person created or operating in the country (see "Mapping of Legal Persons")
- The intended use of each (sub)type of legal person (for example, tax vehicle, nonprofit organization, company)
- The information that is generally available on each (sub)type of legal person
- Law enforcement typologies and case information (both qualitative and quantitative)
- Information relating to suspicious transaction reports involving the different types of legal persons
- The number of tax enforcement cases
- Foreign mutual legal assistance requests involving legal persons (incoming and outgoing)
- The use of legal persons in high- or low-risk sectors or industries
- The strength of mitigating measures such as supervision of CDD requirements
- The legal framework, including the robustness of the requirements to obtain and hold beneficial ownership information

Other factors will need to be considered depending on the risk and context of the country, such as the use of gatekeepers, and the legality and prevalence of foreign and/or politically exposed person ownership of legal persons. Risk indicators should be identified (for example, cross-border activities, the underlying crimes [predicate offenses]) and considered generally and in relation to each type of legal person.

Nonprofit organizations are often legal persons. Although FATF has a separate set of requirements for nonprofit organizations in relation to terrorist financing (Recommendation 8), at the mapping and risk assessment stage, countries should not exclude any type of nonprofit organization that is a legal person (including charities, foundations, or religious entities). It is likely that the risk assessment of nonprofits would focus on risks of abuse of control of the nonprofit organization and its funds. However, as with Recommendation 8 and nonprofit organizations and terrorist financing, Recommendation 24 should not be used to suppress legitimate nongovernmental organizations and their activities. The guidance that FATF issued for Recommendation 8 is applied by extension to Recommendation 24 (FATF 2015).

Consequently, the risks associated with different types of legal person will vary depending on the exact features of each legal person against the country's specific risk profile, even if a type of legal person is known by the same name or title across state or national borders. This also considers that the characteristics and requirements may have changed over time, even if the legal characteristics and intended use of a legal person have a common (legal) origin.

Foreign Legal Persons

Under the revised FATF standards, the risk understanding should also extend to foreign legal persons that present money laundering or terrorist financing risks and have sufficient links with the country (even if they are not created in the country). The rationale for extending this risk assessment requirement follows from the recognition that if foreign legal persons are allowed to operate in or have a presence in a country in the same way as domestic legal persons, then the competent authorities in the country should be equally aware of those risks and take appropriate steps to manage and mitigate them. This mapping exercise should assess how foreign legal persons operate in the country. Countries vary in their openness to foreign legal persons, from barring them from conducting any business activities to allowing them to operate freely. A country's framework for dealing with foreign legal persons should also inform the focus of the mapping exercise, risk assessment, and risk mitigation measures.

Measures to mitigate the risks of foreign legal persons can include requirements for high-risk, foreign-created legal persons to provide their beneficial ownership information directly to authorities in the same way legal persons could be required to share this information (for example, in a registry).

When assessing the risks and designing mitigation measures for legal persons, the country of origin and its beneficial ownership framework are important factors. In this regard, companies incorporated in countries with public beneficial ownership registries, provided the information of the registries is verified and accurate, certainly have an advantage and may need to provide less (or no) information to authorities in their host countries because there is no added value in asking for information that is already publicly available and reliable. The opposite is just as true—companies incorporated in countries that score low on beneficial ownership transparency may need to be subject to additional measures in their host countries. This also applies to transparency of legal arrangements, where these are part of the ownership or control chain of the legal person.

During any mutual evaluation, country officials may inform assessors that certain gaps the assessors may perceive are justified because of low money laundering and terrorist financing risks. Without a risk assessment, however, it appears very difficult to convince the assessors that these arguments are reasonable, especially if the perceived gaps in company law predate the creation of the AML/CFT system.

The following are examples of relevant tests a country could use to determine which types of foreign legal persons present money laundering or terrorist financing risks and have a sufficient link with the country.

Examples of Sufficiency Tests

- *Business activity or permanent establishment.* A country may deem a foreign legal entity to have a sufficient link to the country if it has significant operations (including providing or acquiring good or services) or has a permanent establishment, address, branch, and agency in the country. In some countries, if foreign legal persons offer such services or open establishments, they may already need to be registered with a relevant authority, for example, with the relevant ministries that provide permits for such operations or establishment or a Chamber of Commerce, and so on. Information on the type of foreign legal persons operating could be obtained from those agencies.
- *Business relations.* A foreign legal person may have significant and ongoing business relationships with financial institutions (for example, holding a bank account in the country) or DNFBPs (for example, if they use accounting or legal services). The country could require financial institutions and DNFBPs to provide information on their relationships with foreign legal persons to inform this sufficiency test.
- *Significant assets in country.* A foreign entity can own significant assets in the country. In instances where this asset is registrable (for example, real estate, artwork), the country could determine that the possession of these assets in the country is a sufficient link. A country could source information for this sufficiency test from relevant DNFBPs (for example, real estate agents, art dealers) and registries (for example, land registry).
- *Subject to tax obligations.* A foreign legal entity may be considered to have a sufficient link to the country if it is a resident in the country for tax purposes or subject to tax obligations. Necessary information for this sufficiency test could be sourced from the country's tax authority.
- *Local presence.* A foreign entity may have a local presence through natural persons such as staff, director, or legal owner in the country. For example, in some countries, all foreign incorporated entities that employ any individuals within the country are required to register basic information with the country's company register (FATF 2019).

Examples of Foreign Legal Persons That Present Money Laundering or Terrorist Financing Risks

- *Country risk factors.* A foreign legal person may be considered higher risk as a result of its country of incorporation (for example, foreign legal persons from certain countries designated as not having adequate AML/CFT systems—that is, FATF gray listing) or countries subject to sanctions or embargoes (for example, such as those issued by the United Nations) or designated as posing a higher risk of corruption or terrorist financing risks. A country may also consider taking additional steps to mitigate risks posed by foreign legal persons if their country of residence has a lack of transparency of information (for example, if there are issues in getting access to beneficial ownership information from foreign countries where these legal persons are incorporated).

- *Entity ownership.* Foreign legal persons that are owned or controlled by foreign politically exposed persons could be considered high risk, particularly where these foreign legal persons stem from high-risk countries. The identification of these entity-specific risk factors is dependent on financial institutions and DNFBPs implementing effective CDD systems.

- *Industry risk factors.* The money laundering and terrorist financing risk factors posed by foreign legal persons can also be concentrated in specific sectors. A study by the Organisation for Economic Co-operation and Development found that 19 percent of all cases of foreign bribery identified occurred in the extractives industries (OECD 2014), and public procurement has received increased attention, given its importance during the COVID-19 pandemic. Countries have sought to mitigate these risks by establishing sector-specific public beneficial ownership requirements. For example, several Extractive Industries Transparency Initiative implementing countries have developed extractive industries–specific public beneficial ownership registries and require any legal entities operating in the sector (both domestic and foreign) to disclose their beneficial ownership information (EITI, n.d.). Similarly, certain countries have established public procurement beneficial ownership registers and require any company seeking to compete for government contracts to disclose their beneficial ownership information.

- *Requests for mutual legal assistance.* A country may want to consider if they have received requests for information sharing or mutual legal assistance in the context of foreign investigations for certain types of foreign legal persons that may be operating or present in the country.

Countries are required to take appropriate steps to manage and mitigate the risks that they identified through the risk assessment. Such measures include ensuring that competent authorities have access to information on legal persons and their beneficial owners, including in the context of domestic and foreign investigations. For certain types of foreign legal persons (identified as having high money laundering or terrorist financing risks and a sufficient link to the country), this could include requirements to hold information, including beneficial ownership information about those foreign legal persons within the country itself (Box 2.3).

Box 2.3. Guiding Questions: Risk Assessment of Legal Persons

Types of Risk Assessment

- Has the country carried out a national risk assessment, and does it contain an in-depth assessment of legal persons?
- If not part of the national risk assessment, has the country carried out a legal person's specific or sectoral risk assessment?
- Which authorities/agencies and/or private sector stakeholders participated in the specific or sectoral risk assessment (as part of the national risk assessment or otherwise)?
  - What was the scope of the risk assessment?
    - Does the study extend to all types of legal persons that can be set up in the country? If not, which types of legal persons did the risk assessment cover and not cover?
    - Does the risk assessment consider foreign legal persons that have sufficient links to the country? If so, what type of foreign legal persons did it consider and why?
- How are those conclusions shared with and disseminated to the relevant agencies and authorities and to the private sector (for example, publication, guidance, awareness-raising events)?
- How often is the risk assessment updated?

Methodology

- Did the country use a dedicated methodology?
  - Does the methodology distinguish between money laundering and terrorist financing?
    - What were the sources of information: quantitative versus qualitative (for example, statistics on suspicious transaction reports regarding the misuse of legal persons, financial intelligence unit case studies on the matter, conclusions reached in the national risk assessment or supranational risk assessment)?
    - Are threats and vulnerabilities distinguished adequately?
    - Does the methodology define risk ratings and contain details on how to determine the risk rating?
- Does the risk assessment contain information about the nature and scale of each type of legal person that can be set up in the country, such as the following?
  - Legal framework for each individual type of legal person;
  - Involvement of gatekeepers in the creation of the type of legal entity;
  - Lawful purposes (commercial and noncommercial) for which the type of legal person can be used or is usually used;
  - Limitations to the use of the type of legal person (that is, certain types of lawful activities in which the legal person cannot engage);
  - How common the type of legal person is, including the overall number and relative importance;
  - Information on the availability of basic information and how it can be accessed;
  - Information on the availability of beneficial ownership information, including the sources (for example, central register) and how it can be accessed; and

(Continued)

Box 2.3. Continued

- The basis for including certain types of foreign legal persons in the risk assessment (criteria used to determine sufficiency links)?
- Does the risk assessment describe in sufficient detail the various scenarios of misuse of individual types of legal persons for money laundering or terrorist financing purposes?
  - Does it distinguish between domestic and international threats? Does the study identify a set of risk indicators (for example, cross-border activities, the use of cash, predicate offenses) with reference to the national risk assessment and/or other relevant risk assessments?
  - Do these allow for an adequate reflection of risk variations between different types of legal persons?
  - Is there a specific focus on the risk associated with the intervention of gatekeepers?
  - Does it address the risks related to third-party introducers?
  - Does it address the risks associated with nominee shareholders and directors?
  - Does it address the risks associated with bearer shares and bearer share warrants?
  - Is there a specific focus on the risk associated with foreign ownership?
  - Are data sufficiently detailed to identify the largest source countries for foreign ownership?
- What are the mitigation measures in place? A nonexhaustive list of examples of mitigation measures includes (and consideration should be given to the adequacy of these measures and whether there are any deficiencies that should be addressed):
  - The legal framework, including filing of basic and beneficial ownership information;
  - Accessible registers with basic and beneficial ownership information by FIs/DNFBPs and/or general public;
  - Supervisory efforts to ensure that legal requirements are implemented adequately (for example, oversight measures to ensure that legal persons obtain and hold information on their beneficial owners through an up-to-date register to be kept, if any, and file changes in a timely manner);
  - Anti–money laundering and combating the financing of terrorism (AML/CFT) preventive measures for obliged entities, including adequate beneficial ownership requirements; and
  - AML/CFT supervisory measures to ensure effective implementation of AML/CFT preventive measures by obliged entities.
- Does the risk assessment arrive at a residual risk rating, taking mitigation measures into account?
- What are the risk assessment's conclusions regarding residual money laundering and terrorist financing risks?

Foreign Legal Persons

- Has the country conducted a risk assessment that considers foreign legal persons with a sufficient link to the country?
- What factors were used to identify foreign legal persons with a sufficient link?
- What factors are considered with respect to risks of foreign legal persons with a sufficient link to the country?

REFERENCES

Armour, John, Henry Hansmann, and Reinier Kraakman. 2009. "The Essential Elements of Corporate Law: What Is Corporate Law?" Harvard John M. Olin Discussion Paper Series No. 643; Harvard John M. Olin Center for Law, Economics, and Business; Cambridge, MA. http://www.law.harvard.edu/programs/olin_center/papers/pdf/Kraakman_643.pdf.

Basel Committee on Banking Supervision. 2012. "Core Principles for Effective Banking Supervision." Bank for International Settlements, Basel, Switzerland. https://www.bis.org/publ/bcbs230.pdf.

Doublet, Yves-Marie. 2011. "Political Funding: Thematic Review of GRECO's Third Evaluation Round." Group of States against Corruption, Strasbourg, France. https://rm.coe.int/16806cbff2.

European Central Bank. 2021. *Guide to Fit and Proper Assessments*. Frankfurt: European Central Bank. https://www.bankingsupervision.europa.eu/ecb/pub/pdf/ssm.fit_and_proper_guide_update202112-d66f230eca.en.pdf.

Extractive Industries Transparency Initiative (EITI). 2019. *The EITI Standard 2019*. Oslo: EITI International Secretariat. https://eiti.org/sites/default/files/attachments/eiti_standard2019_a4_en.pdf.

Extractive Industries Transparency Initiative (EITI). n.d. "Beneficial Ownership: Knowing Who Owns and Controls Extractive Companies." https://eiti.org/beneficial-ownership.

Financial Action Task Force (FATF). 2006. "The Misuse of Corporate Vehicles, Including Trust and Company Service Providers." Financial Action Task Force, Paris. https://www.fatf-gafi.org/media/fatf/documents/reports/Misuse%20of%20Corporate%20Vehicles%20including%20Trusts%20and%20Company%20Services%20Providers.pdf.

Financial Action Task Force (FATF). 2012. *International Standards on Combating Money Laundering and the Financing of Terrorism and Proliferation, updated March 2022*. Paris: Financial Action Task Force. https://www.fatf-gafi.org/media/fatf/documents/recommendations/pdfs/FATF%20Recommendations%202012.pdf.

Financial Action Task Force (FATF). 2013. "National Money Laundering and Terrorist Financing Risk Assessment." Financial Action Task Force, Paris. http://www.fatf-gafi.org/media/fatf/content/images/National_ML_TF_Risk_Assessment.pdf.

Financial Action Task Force (FATF). 2014. "Guidance on Transparency and Beneficial Ownership." Financial Action Task Force, Paris. https://www.fatf-gafi.org/media/fatf/documents/reports/Guidance-transparency-beneficial-ownership.pdf.

Financial Action Task Force (FATF). 2015. "Combating the Abuse of Nonprofit Organizations (Recommendation 8)." Financial Action Task Force, Paris. https://www.fatf-gafi.org/media/fatf/documents/reports/BPP-combating-abuse-non-profit-organisations.pdf.

Financial Action Task Force (FATF). 2019. "Best Practices on Beneficial Ownership for Legal Persons." Financial Action Task Force, Paris. https://www.fatf-gafi.org/media/fatf/documents/Best-Practices-Beneficial-Ownership-Legal-Persons.pdf.

Financial Action Task Force (FATF). 2022. "Report on the State of Effectiveness Compliance with FATF Standards." FATF, Paris. https://www.fatf-gafi.org/media/fatf/documents/recommendations/Report-on-the-State-of-Effectiveness-Compliance-with-FATF-Standards.pdf.

Financial Action Task Force (FATF). n.d. "Glossary of the FATF Recommendations." https://www.fatf-gafi.org/glossary/.

Financial Action Task Force and Egmont Group of Financial Intelligence Units (FATF and Egmont Group). 2018. "Concealment of Beneficial Ownership." Financial Action Task Force and Egmont Group, Paris. https://www.fatf-gafi.org/media/fatf/documents/reports/FATF-Egmont-Concealment-beneficial-ownership.pdf.

Financial Action Task Force and Egmont Group of Financial Intelligence Units (FATF and Egmont Group). 2020. "Trade-Based Money Laundering: Trends and Developments." Financial Action Task Force and Egmont Group, Paris. https://www.fatf-gafi.org/media/fatf/content/Trade-Based-Money-Laundering-Trends-and-Developments.pdf.

Group of Twenty (G20). 2014. "G20 High-Level Principles on Beneficial Ownership Transparency." Group of Twenty, Australia. http://www.g20.utoronto.ca/2014/g20_high-level_principles_beneficial_ownership_transparency.pdf.

Global Forum on Transparency and Exchange of Information for Tax Purposes and Inter-American Development Bank (Global Forum and IDB). 2019. *A Beneficial Ownership Implementation Toolkit.* Washington, DC, and Paris: Inter-American Development Bank and Organisation for Economic Co-operation and Development. https://publications.iadb.org /publications/english/document/A_Beneficial_Ownership_Implementation_Toolkit _en_en.pdf.

O'Halloran, Kerry. 2012. *The Profits of Charity: International Perspectives on the Law Governing the Involvement of Charities in Commerce.* New York: Oxford University Press.

Organisation for Economic Co-operation and Development (OECD). 2001. *Behind the Corporate Veil: Using Corporate Entities for Illicit Purposes.* Paris: Organisation for Economic Co-operation and Development. https://www.oecd.org/daf/ca/43703185.pdf.

Organisation for Economic Co-operation and Development (OECD). 2014. *Foreign Bribery Report: An Analysis of the Crime of Bribery of Foreign Public Officials.* Paris: OECD Publishing. https://read.oecd-ilibrary.org/governance/oecd-foreign-bribery-report_9789264226616 -en#page1.

Organisation for Economic Co-operation and Development (OECD). 2021. *Ending the Shell Game Cracking Down on the Professionals Who Enable Tax and White Collar Crimes.* Paris: Organisation for Economic Co-operation and Development. https://www.oecd.org/tax /crime/ending-the-shell-game-cracking-down-on-the-professionals-who-enable-tax-and -white-collar-crime.pdf.

United Nations (UN). 2015a. "Midterm Report of the Panel of Experts Established Pursuant to Resolution 1874 (2009)." UN document reference S/2017/742, United Nations, New York. https://documents-dds-ny.un.org/doc/UNDOC/GEN/N17/246/50/PDF/N1724650 .pdf?OpenElement.

United Nations (UN). 2015b. "Report of the Panel of Experts Established Pursuant to Resolution 1874 (2009)." UN document reference S/2015/131, United Nations, New York. https://www .securitycouncilreport.org/atf/cf/%7B65BFCF9B-6D27-4E9C-8CD3-CF6E4FF96FF9%7D/s _2015_131.pdf.

United Nations Office on Drugs and Crime (UNODC). 2009. "Technical Guidance to the United Nations Convention against Corruption." https://www.unodc.org/documents/treaties /UNCAC/Publications/TechnicalGuide/09-84395_Ebook.pdf.

United Nations Office on Drugs and Crime and World Bank (UNODC and World Bank). 2007. *Stolen Asset Recovery (StAR) Initiative: Challenges, Opportunities, and Action Plan.* Washington DC: World Bank. https://www.unodc.org/pdf/Star_Report.pdf.

US Department of Justice (DOJ). 2017. "Acting Manhattan US Attorney Announces Historic Jury Verdict Finding Forfeiture of Midtown Office Building and Other Properties." News release 17-200, June 29, 2017. https://www.justice.gov/usao-sdny/pr/acting-manhattan -us-attorney-announces-historic-jury-verdict-finding-forfeiture-midtown.

van der Does de Willebois, Emile, Emily M. Halter, Robert A. Harrison, Ji Won Park, and J. C. Sharman. 2011. *Puppet Masters: How the Corrupt Use Legal Structures to Hide Stolen Assets and What to Do about It.* Washington DC: World Bank. https://openknowledge.world bank.org/bitstream/handle/10986/2363/9780821388945.pdf?sequence=6&isAllowed=y.

Wolfsberg Group. 2012a. "The Wolfsberg AML Principles Frequently Asked Questions with Regard to Beneficial Ownership in the Context of Private Banking." Wolfsberg Group, Ermatingen, Switzerland. https://www.wolfsberg-principles.com/sites/default/files/wb/pdfs /faqs/19.%20Wolfsberg-FAQs-on-Beneficial-Ownership-May-2012.pdf.

Wolfsberg Group. 2012b. "Wolfsberg Anti–Money Laundering Principles for Private Banking." Wolfsberg Group, Ermatingen, Switzerland. https://www.wolfsberg-principles.com/sites /default/files/wb/pdfs/wolfsberg-standards/10.%20Wolfsberg-Private-Banking-Prinicples -May-2012.pdf.

CHAPTER 3

Practical Implementation of Beneficial Ownership Requirements

Policymakers should try to gain a thorough understanding of the common practical challenges to meeting international requirements on updating records on beneficial ownership over the lifespan of a legal person. The starting point is to understand the strengths and weaknesses of information sources when refining procedures for making them adequate, accurate, and up to date. Best practices then lead the way.

This chapter distills the concept of beneficial ownership, including key considerations such as what it means for beneficial ownership information to be accurate, adequate, and up to date. It also looks at the different ways in which beneficial ownership information can be obtained and held, and how the Financial Action Task Force (FATF) requirements for beneficial ownership might be applied during the typical life cycle of a legal person (from creation to dissolution). It also sets out the various broad policy considerations that countries should factor in when setting up or reviewing a beneficial ownership regime.

KEY CONCEPTS OF BENEFICIAL OWNERSHIP

Adequate Beneficial Ownership Information

The concept of beneficial ownership is different from legal ownership and requires an in-depth understanding of the notions related to both "ownership" and "control."

Adequate information is information that is sufficient to identify the natural person(s) who are the beneficial owner(s) and the means and mechanisms through which they exercise beneficial ownership or control.
—FATF Recommendation 24

To understand the concept of beneficial ownership, it is important to understand who is the beneficial owner and why or how they are the beneficial owner—that is, the means and mechanisms by which they own and/or exert control over a legal person. This requires an understanding of notions related to both ownership and control.

At a very basic level, beneficial ownership is determined by factors such as the number of shares that a natural person may hold in a legal person. Countries may choose to impose a qualifying ownership threshold (for example, a maximum of 25 percent) that might help to identify beneficial ownership, though this is not always straightforward. Control, however, can be determined by other factors (for example, which natural person can make decisions in relation to a legal person). Competent authorities should also understand that identifying who controls the legal person is not always the same as determining who owns the legal person or who owns a certain threshold of shares in it.

A common misconception is that knowing the shareholders of a company is sufficient to determine who the beneficial owners are. However, shareholders can include other legal persons. In addition, even if the shareholder information refers to natural persons, it still does not always consider natural persons who may exercise control over the legal structure without necessarily being shareholders. It also does not reflect those shareholders who may have control over the legal person because of the type of shares they hold, in contrast to ownership thresholds.

Common Practical Challenges

Various practical issues can be encountered in dealing with different types of legal persons, including the nature of shares and the way that ownership and/or control is exerted on the legal person. The following is a nonexhaustive overview of some of the common practical challenges that may be encountered when trying to identify ownership and/or control of a legal person.

Complex ownership and control structures. Complex legal structures can be created and exist for legitimate purposes, but the more complex they are (for example, multiple layers of ownership, spread across jurisdictions), the more difficult it is for competent authorities to identify who owns and/or controls the structure. However, even the most complex structure exists for a reason, and that reason should be understood (for example, by a bank taking on a legal person as a customer, or by a trust and company service provider [TCSP] forming the legal person). If there is no adequate explanation for the use of a complex legal structure, this could indicate that the company structure is deliberately complex to disguise the beneficial owner, or it may have been created to facilitate or commit a crime—and the relevant authority should treat this as a red flag.

Ownership thresholds. For practical purposes related to carrying out customer due diligence (CDD), countries often put thresholds in place for identifying beneficial owners regarding ownership levels (for example, 10 percent or 25 percent shareholdings). Share ownership above these thresholds can sometimes indicate beneficial ownership but is not necessarily the only determining factor in ascertaining the beneficial owner.

Legal persons can be vastly different from one another, and applying one threshold does not adequately capture the different ownership structures of these different legal entities. If thresholds are imposed, they should be set proportionate to the risk posed by the type of legal person. For example, a legal person that presents no particular risk factors might justify a maximum of 25 percent threshold (the FATF standards' suggested maximum threshold), whereas higher-risk situations might warrant a lower threshold or even no threshold (FATF 2012).[1] Lower thresholds mean that more potential beneficial owners will be found. Lower thresholds are particularly relevant in relation to fit and proper requirements for ownership of financial institutions.

Furthermore, any threshold—regardless of how low it has been set—can be circumvented through exercising control of the legal person. Countries should clarify this in the legal framework and issue appropriate guidance to ensure that countries adopt a comprehensive definition of beneficial ownership that includes both concepts of ownership and control.

At some point, the number of shareholders might also dilute ownership enough that identifying each separate beneficial owner would not be possible and would create too heavy an administrative burden. The standards recognize that if ownership is so diversified that there are no natural persons (whether acting alone or together) exercising control of the legal person through ownership, then control through "other means" should be examined. Other means might include holding a significant influence function or being closely related to a shareholder and/or being able to exert influence on them. This may be the case for certain publicly traded companies.

Voting rights. Shareholder voting rights might be an indication of beneficial ownership because in theory, the power to direct the affairs of the legal person should lie ultimately in the hands of the voting shareholders. However, not all legal persons issue shares with voting rights or with equal voting rights. For example, a company might allow shareholders one vote per share, thus giving those with higher equity in the company more votes. Other companies might allocate one vote per shareholder, thus giving minority shareholders or groups of minority shareholders a bigger say in the company's affairs than their equity stake would otherwise suggest.

Golden shares. Golden shares traditionally give the holder a majority of the voting rights, which means that the holder can outvote all other shareholders, and this often results in giving their holders effective control over the company. Although many such shares were originally given to governments after privatization of state-owned companies, their wider use could give a distorted view of control if the simple value of shares was viewed as the basis for ascertaining beneficial ownership information.

Nominee shareholders and directors. Legal persons that allow nominees to represent shareholders and directors can be misused by those trying to hide beneficial ownership information. Some nominee arrangements are legitimate and formal in nature (for example, governed by a written contract and disclosed to the legal person), but others can involve less formal or more opaque arrangements, in which the nominee is used primarily to conceal the beneficial owner's identity. (See this chapter's "Nominee Shareholders and Directors" section for a broader discussion of relevant issues.)

---

[1] The revised FATF standards suggest that controlling shareholders may be based on a threshold, but that this should be determined based on the jurisdiction's assessment of risk and be set with a maximum of 25 percent.

Undisclosed agent arrangements. Those seeking beneficial ownership information should be conscious of business and other relationships that may suggest that a director or shareholder is acting as an agent for another person. For example, a person may hold shares or a directorship in a company, but also be an employee of another person or company. It may be that the director or shareholder is acting at the behest of the controller of the company in which he is employed. This could also be a type of nominee arrangement.

Family members and other strawmen. The use of strawmen in such arrangements can be particularly challenging and can be a nominee arrangement. In such cases, the ownership and formal control of a legal person will be with a person that is (closely) related to or associated with another person. The fact that the true control may be with another person may be evident by the nature of the relationship between the legal owner and the actual beneficial owner, such as an (unequal) family relationship (for example, parent-child), an (unequal) professional relationship (for example, former employee-employer), or another link (for example, former colleagues). Another clue is the fact that the legal owner seems to have had no means to acquire the legal entity or has little (professional) experience to justify owning a company. This type of relationship between the legal and beneficial owner is especially prevalent in relation to politically exposed persons (PEPs), and FATF's guidance provides more details in this area (FATF 2013a).

Publicly traded companies. The international standards acknowledge that being listed on a stock exchange already imposes sufficient transparency requirements that would enable a financial institution or designated nonfinancial business and profession (DNFBP) to accept information that is in a public register or available from the customer or from another reliable source. However, this provision's usefulness will depend partly on the completeness and reliability of the relevant country's company listing process, which would need to be enforced robustly.

Foreign legal persons. Where foreign legal persons are part of the chain of ownership of a legal person, challenges in accessing beneficial ownership information from host countries arise if countries do not have beneficial ownership information publicly available, do not register beneficial ownership information at all, or have a track record of not sharing accurate beneficial ownership information with other countries promptly. In addition, when relying on the information that can be accessed on a beneficial ownership register in another jurisdiction, consideration should be given to this information's reliability (for example, whether the country has a weak regime for anti–money laundering and combating the financing of terrorism [AML/CFT]). Related to this, countries should consider additional measures where foreign legal persons have significant control/ownership of a legal person, such as requiring that beneficial ownership information of that foreign legal person be held in the country.

Figure 3.1 shows how legal ownership can be widespread, but by looking far enough up the ownership chain, the real beneficial owner can be traced by applying two tests: ownership (in this case, using ownership thresholds of up to 25 percent) and control.

The ownership interests in Company A are as follows:

Figure 3.1. Example of Complex Structure

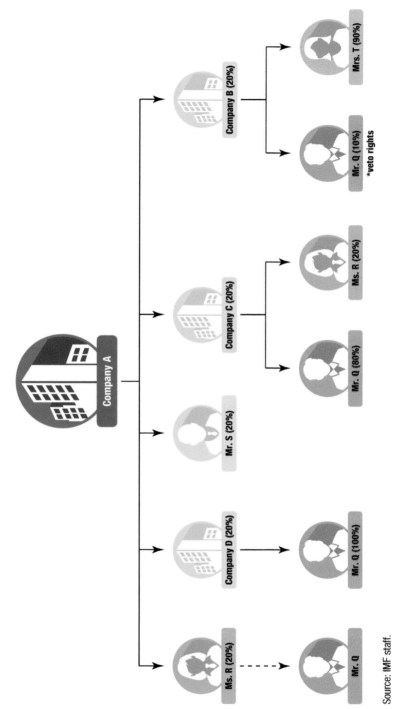

Source: IMF staff.

Mrs. T. has 18 percent (she owns 90 percent of Company B, which owns 20 percent of Company A).

Ms. R. has 24 percent (she owns 20 percent of Company A directly and 20 percent of Company C, which owns 20 percent of Company A).

Mr. S. directly owns 20 percent of Company A.

Mr. Q. owns 38 percent (he owns 100 percent of Company D, which owns 20 percent of Company A and 80 percent of Company C [which owns 20 percent of Company A and 10 percent of Company B, which owns 20 percent of Company A]). Thus, by applying an ownership threshold of 25 percent, Mr. Q. is the beneficial owner of Company A. In addition, if the control structure of Company A was examined further (beyond ownership interest), Mr. Q. holds veto rights for decision-making processes in Company B, even though he owns only 10 percent of this company, and he also controls Ms. R. indirectly (who happens to be his daughter and a nominee shareholder). Mr. Q. therefore is a key beneficial owner with direct and indirect ownership and control of this legal structure.

Countries should also consider what constitutes adequate information to establish the identity of the beneficial owner or owners, for example, types of personal data and supporting documentation. The definition of adequate information includes, for example, the full name, nationality or nationalities, the full date and place of birth, residential address, national identification number and document type, and the tax identification number or equivalent in the country of residence. The types of information that should be collected to determine ownership and control are discussed in the next section.

Accurate Beneficial Ownership Information

A risk-based approach to verification is helpful to ensure that beneficial ownership is accurate.

Accurate information is information which has been verified to confirm its accuracy by verifying the identity and status of the beneficial owner using reliable, independently sourced/obtained documents, data, or information. The extent of verification measures may vary according to the specific level of risk. Countries should consider complementary measures as necessary to support the accuracy of beneficial ownership information e.g., discrepancy reporting.
—FATF Recommendation 24

Information should be subject to a certain degree of verification to determine whether it is accurate. Such verification could be done using a risk-based approach that considers the specific country context, the money laundering or terrorist financing risks presented by various legal entities that operate within the country (based on the risk assessment), and the type and complexity of the legal structure.

A risk-based approach to verification can be set up along the following lines. At a minimum, countries should require that information provided on the identity of the beneficial owner is validated against original source documents, such as passports and other forms of official identification. Some of this information might be the same as the basic information collected when a company is set up (if the shareholder is indeed the beneficial owner).

Following a risk-based approach, simple corporate structures or corporate structures that a country has identified as low risk would not require more detailed verification checks, aside from ensuring that the documents presented are authentic and up to date. More complex legal structures and those identified as high risk (even if they are simple structures on the face of it, such as shell companies) could require more sources for verifying the information presented, including a greater focus on documents establishing the beneficial owners' status (for example, shareholder documents, other agreements providing natural persons with control over the legal arrangement). A more detailed verification would require different lines of inquiry, possible cross-referencing of data with other databases and competent authorities, and a comprehensive understanding of the legal structure and the reasons as to why the structure has been set up.

Depending on the mechanism for holding this information, verification responsibilities will need to be imposed on the relevant public authority or body collecting the beneficial ownership information, including to ensure that they have appropriate powers, funding, resources, and technical capacity to carry out the verification. Provision for this mandate and resources should be clear in the relevant legal and regulatory frameworks.

Where beneficial ownership information is available publicly or can be cross-referenced by other stakeholders (that is, banks and other businesses and professions that may also collect this information as part of their CDD obligations), these stakeholders should also be able to report discrepancies, which can also help support ongoing information verification. Where beneficial ownership information is publicly available, civil society and others can play a role in reporting discrepancies because they might be interested in investigating legal structures.

Up-to-Date Beneficial Ownership Information

Up-to-date information is information which is as current and up-to-date as possible and is updated within a reasonable period (e.g., within one month) following any change.
—FATF Recommendation 24

The requirement that beneficial ownership information is up to date requires that measures should be in place to ensure that the information is current and updated within a reasonable period (for example, a month or less) when any changes are made to this information. Depending on how a country holds beneficial ownership information, the time frame to update could be shorter or even real time. For example, if a gatekeeper (such as a TCSP, notary, accountant, or lawyer) is responsible for setting up a company and holds beneficial ownership information for it, they should be responsible for updating this information at the same time that changes are made with respect to the beneficial owners.

These requirements should be imposed by law with appropriate sanctions for failure to provide updated information. In addition, countries should also consider requiring higher-risk legal persons to declare their beneficial ownership information to the relevant authorities regularly (for example, annually) to ensure that the authority holds accurate information.

Having up-to-date information does not mean that a record of the previous beneficial owners should be erased. It is equally important for authorities and other authorized or relevant parties to have access to information on past beneficial owners (as discussed in this chapter's "Public Authority/Body Holding Beneficial Ownership Information or an Alternative Mechanism" section). Such records can prove very useful, particularly in the context of investigations in which legal persons' ownership and/or controls structures might have been changed on purpose.

SOURCES/MECHANISMS FOR BENEFICIAL OWNERSHIP INFORMATION

> *Countries should adopt a multipronged approach for obtaining and holding beneficial ownership information and ensure that this information is available to competent authorities timely and efficiently.*

Countries should consider several different mechanisms and frameworks for obtaining and holding up-to-date beneficial ownership information. The standards require that countries use all the following sources and mechanisms, including requiring (1) information to be held by the companies themselves, (2) information to be held by a public authority or body (for example, tax authority, financial intelligence unit [FIU], companies' registry, or beneficial ownership registry) or an alternative mechanism, and (3) using additional supplementary measures such as information obtained by financial institutions, professional gatekeepers, and DNFBPs (Figure 3.2).

Under the multipronged approach, countries need to ensure that beneficial ownership information is available from all these sources and that they cannot choose just one option, as the original standards allowed. This is one of the most significant changes that was proposed in the revisions to Recommendation 24 in March 2022.

Figure 3.2. Sources and Mechanisms for Beneficial Ownership Information

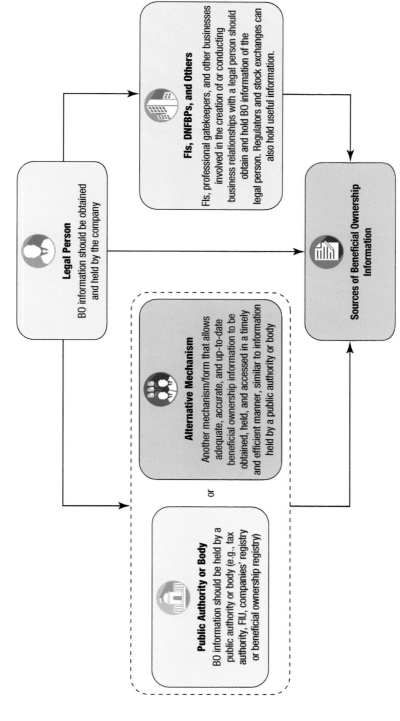

Legal Person

BO information should be obtained and held by the company

FIs, DNFBPs, and Others

FIs, professional gatekeepers, and other businesses involved in the creation of or conducting business relationships with a legal person should obtain and hold BO information of the legal person. Regulators and stock exchanges can also hold useful information.

Alternative Mechanism

Another mechanism/form that allows adequate, accurate, and up-to-date beneficial ownership information to be obtained, held, and accessed in a timely and efficient manner, similar to information held by a public authority or body

or

Public Authority or Body

BO information should be held by a public authority or body (e.g., tax authority, FIU, companies' registry or beneficial ownership registry)

Sources of Beneficial Ownership Information

Sources: Financial Action Task Force; and IMF staff.
Note: BO = beneficial ownership; DNFBP = designated nonfinancial business and professions; FI = financial institution; FIU = financial intelligence unit.

The need to implement a multipronged approach became evidently clear based on the results of the ongoing FATF fourth-round mutual evaluations. The evaluations proved that most countries have considerable challenges in effectively holding adequate, accurate, and up-to-date beneficial ownership information, especially if they relied on only one or two sources of beneficial ownership information (for example, several countries have depended on beneficial ownership information that was collected as part of CDD measures, but this has proven an ineffective source on its own). No country has managed to achieve a rating of highly effective yet, and only very few countries have achieved a rating of substantial effectiveness for Immediate Outcome 5 (and in such cases, most of them relied on more than one information source and/or had a centralized register for beneficial ownership). This was also reflected in FATF's Best Practices on Beneficial Ownership for Legal Persons paper (FATF 2019), which highlighted that "a multipronged approach using several sources of information is often more effective in preventing the misuse of legal persons for criminal purposes and implementing measures that make the beneficial ownership of legal persons sufficiently transparent."

Legal Persons Holding Information on Their Beneficial Owners

Legal persons should be aware of their own structures and know their beneficial owners. Unwillingness or inability to declare their beneficial owner or owners should raise red flags.

Overview

A legal person should know who owns and controls it. Even in cases involving complicated legal structures, legitimate structures will be knowingly set up for a specific purpose, probably using specific structures (for example, tax planning). This means that those who create and/or administer the structure should also be able to provide accurate beneficial ownership information.

Therefore, when countries rely on legal persons and their representatives to obtain and hold beneficial ownership information, the requirement for them to do so should be clearly set out in law or enforceable means. The requirement to hold this information should apply not just to all legal persons in the future but also to all legal persons currently in existence and operating in a country.

It also follows that all legal persons must know their beneficial owners to be able to provide this information up front to the relevant public authority/body, financial institutions, and others in the context of CDD measures and to share this information with other competent authorities in a timely manner. If legal persons are unwilling or unable to provide this information or there are concerns regarding the accuracy of the information provided, then this could be a reason to not allow legal entities to be created or continue to exist or to form/maintain business relationships.

Challenges can arise when countries have legal persons that use complex structures (for example, involving multiple layers); have parts of the ownership and/or control structures in another jurisdiction; are subject to frequent changes regarding structure, legal, and beneficial ownership; or allow their beneficial ownership information to be held by a third-party professional who may use legal or professional privilege as a barrier to providing the information.

Under the earlier versions of the FATF standards, legal persons were permitted to have their beneficial ownership information held by third parties, typically lawyers, notaries, and other types of TCSPs, often operating in other jurisdictions. However, allowing third parties to hold such information and/or holding information in third countries proved particularly challenging with respect to timely access to this information. It also made it more difficult to verify the information for accuracy because sometimes third parties would attempt to use legal privilege, financial secrecy, or data protection rules to shield some or all information that would otherwise be necessary to accurately identify or verify the beneficial ownership. Additional challenges arose where such third parties were not subject to AML/CFT obligations in their home jurisdiction and therefore would not be under a legal obligation to maintain these records or were not subject to stringent supervision, affecting the quality of the information they held.

These gaps are now addressed under the revised FATF standards because legal persons are now required to obtain and hold their beneficial ownership information and to cooperate with competent authorities to the fullest extent possible in determining the beneficial owner, and this information is also expected to be registered within a country through a public authority/body or alternative mechanism.

The unwillingness or inability of a legal person's representatives to explain their structure and their beneficial owners can be a red flag for potential suspicion of money laundering or terrorist financing for any competent authority or business (for example, a bank) that establishes or maintains a customer relationship. The caveat to this is that in some cases, beneficial ownership information may be *temporarily* confidential—for example, certain information might be sensitive during acquisitions and mergers. However, confidentiality and need-to-know principles do not justify a *permanent* lack of information or an inability to explain.

Legal persons should have the power to request information from their shareholders, even though shareholder information alone will often not be sufficient to prove the identity of the beneficial owner. To support legal persons in holding accurate information on their beneficial owners, competent authorities should issue guidance to assist the legal person in identifying who the beneficial owner might be, bearing in mind that the concept is different from the shareholder information to which legal persons might be more accustomed. If a competent authority wanted to obtain more recent beneficial ownership information from the legal person itself, then there is a danger (for example, in the case of law enforcement investigations) that approaching the legal person could alert its officials or shareholders that an investigation is underway. Therefore, countries should also impose a requirement that the legal person cooperate with the competent authorities to the fullest extent to determine the beneficial owner (without alerting or tipping off the beneficial owner in the context of ongoing investigations) and that the legal person should have one or more natural persons resident in the country to be accountable to the competent authorities (Box 3.1). See Guiding Questions for Legal Persons (Box 3.2).

Box 3.1. Implementation Guidance: Enforceable Provisions and Sanctions

The following is a summary of the enforceable provisions and sanctions that countries should consider including in their legal framework.

Power to request information from shareholders. Countries should ensure that the legal person has the legal power to request beneficial ownership and related supporting information from their shareholders (without having to provide justification) and that they have the power to take appropriate action (for example, suspension of voting rights or removal of directors/shareholders) if the information is not provided or is inaccurate.

Timely access to information by competent authorities. Countries should establish clear expectations/timelines for legal persons to share beneficial ownership information with competent authorities and to cooperate with them as much as possible. This should be done on request and as soon as possible (for example, within 24 hours once the request has been made), which should not be an issue because the information is expected to be available in the country. In addition, competent authorities should not have to provide justification for requesting this information to avoid tipping off the beneficial owner in the context of ongoing investigations.

Tipping off. Appropriate sanctions should be imposed when legal persons are found to have tipped off the beneficial owner, for example, fines against the legal person. In extreme cases, striking the legal person from the company registry should be considered.

Provision of information to financial institutions and designated nonfinancial businesses and professions (DNFBPs). Countries should require legal persons to share beneficial ownership information with financial institutions and DNFBPs with which they have relationships. When legal persons or their representatives appear to be unwilling to disclose their beneficial ownership, competent authorities should consider not allowing such legal persons to operate in their jurisdiction, and financial institutions and DNFBPs should apply enhanced scrutiny of the business relationship and consider refraining from doing business with such legal persons and filing a suspicious transaction report.

Box 3.2. Guiding Questions: Legal Persons

- Is there a legal requirement for legal persons to obtain and hold adequate, accurate, and up-to-date information on their beneficial ownership?
  - Does it extend to all legal persons that can be created/incorporated/registered in the country? If not, what are the reasons for the exemptions, and are these justifiable?
  - Are there legal provisions to ensure that this also applies to all legal persons that are currently in existence and operating in a country and not just new legal persons that are to be created/incorporated/registered in the country?
  - Is there guidance for legal persons on the implementation of the requirement?
    - Does it include a definition and background information on the concept of beneficial ownership?
    - Is this information also held by gatekeepers (for example, trust and company service providers)?
    - Do legal persons have unrestricted power to request this information from shareholders?
- Are legal persons required to keep beneficial ownership up to date, reflecting any changes within a reasonable period (for example, within one month or sooner)?
- Do legal persons maintain records of previous changes to ownership structures?
- What sanctioning measures are taken for failure to obtain and hold beneficial ownership information?
  - Can the legal person be held liable for failure to implement the requirement?
    - Who in the legal person can be held liable for failure to implement the requirement? What about when ownership and management are completely nonresident?
  - Are sanctions effective, proportionate, and dissuasive?
  - How is it ensured that failures are addressed following a sanction?
- What are the mechanisms in place to ensure that competent authorities can get timely access to the beneficial ownership information kept by the legal person?
  - Is there any guidance for competent authorities on their access to beneficial ownership information kept by/on behalf of legal persons?
  - Are legal persons required to cooperate fully with competent authorities, including by making their beneficial ownership information available in a timely manner (for example, within 24 hours upon request)?
  - How quickly can the information be obtained (on average)?
  - Are there any legal requirements and related sanctions to prevent legal persons from tipping off beneficial owners if competent authorities request this information?
- What are the mechanisms in place to ensure that legal persons provide financial institutions and designated nonfinancial businesses and professions with adequate, accurate, and up-to-date beneficial ownership information?

Public Authority/Body Holding Beneficial Ownership Information or an Alternative Mechanism

Regardless of who holds information or how it is held, the guiding principles should be that the information is accurate, adequate, up to date, and accessible in a timely manner. Effectiveness can be demonstrated by adherence to these key principles, regardless of the form/mechanism in which the information is held.

Having a public authority or body—such as an FIU, tax authority, or other relevant competent authority—hold this information is a way to ensure that the relevant competent authorities have access to this information timely and efficiently. The way that this information is held can vary from authority/body (for example, registry format or another type of relevant database), but the key principles remain: that the information should be collected (or there should be an obligation for legal persons or gatekeepers, where applicable, to provide this information to the relevant authority upon creation and when changes occur) and that this information should be verified so that it is adequate, accurate, and up to date. Another key consideration is that regardless of which public authority holds this information, it should be easily and rapidly accessible to other competent authorities for their use and not restricted in any way.

Of these options, holding the information in a registry format (either as part of the company registry or in other existing registries or having a separate beneficial ownership registry) is the preferred option. This section focuses primarily on the considerations necessary for implementing a registry approach, noting that registries can take different shapes and forms, including to be held in the form of multiple registries or databases (for example, separate registries for provinces, districts, sectors, or specific types of legal person).

If countries choose to adopt an alternative mechanism, such a mechanism should follow similar considerations, namely, to ensure efficient access to adequate, accurate, and up-to-date beneficial ownership information. It is not yet clear what could be an alternative mechanism under the revised FATF standards. This will be determined on a case-by-case basis according to countries' individual circumstances and will likely include other types of formats/mechanisms not contemplated in this guide.

If a country adopts an alternative mechanism, the onus will fall on the country to demonstrate to the assessors in the context of AML/CFT mutual evaluations how this mechanism meets the requirements of the standards. Without any current examples of this, we note that the considerations set out for the registry approach (taking a broad understanding of what a registry could be) should apply to the same extent possible for an alternative mechanism. If countries choose an alternative approach, this will put an added burden on the country to demonstrate its effectiveness to assessors as part of their mutual evaluation, and other countries that may want to access information on a particular legal person or otherwise seek international cooperation from that country. They will need to demonstrate that it is just as efficient as the registry format. Examples of what might entail alternative mechanisms may be elaborated through FATF guidance and are likely to become clearer as countries are assessed against the new standards.

Countries should assess what registry mechanism/form will provide competent authorities with the most efficient access to information by considering the specific country's risk, context, and materiality. To the extent possible, countries should be able to explain why they adopted a specific mechanism/form and document this decision, also for the purpose of explaining this during their AML/CFT assessment. For example, countries with more advanced corporate structures or in which a high number of legal structures tend to be incorporated or operate should certainly consider adopting a registry approach held either by the companies' registry, or as a separate beneficial ownership registry.

Registry Approach

Holding beneficial ownership in a centralized repository (a registry or similar type of database) is the most effective way to ensure that there is timely and efficient access to beneficial ownership information.

Overview

Registries holding beneficial ownership information are a good way to centralize access to beneficial ownership information and allow competent authorities to have timely and efficient access to this information. Such beneficial ownership registries can be stand-alone or built upon existing databases (such as company registries that are maintained by or for an incorporating authority) and hold basic information (that is, information about legal ownership) of companies incorporated or licensed in the country.

The international standards do not prescribe which public authority should be tasked with the registration and ensuring the accuracy of beneficial ownership information, and the appropriate solution will differ from one country to another. Examples of possible government entities that can hold such registries are company or commercial registrars, ministries of justice, FIUs, and tax authorities.

Where other authorities are to hold beneficial ownership information (for example, tax authorities), countries should ensure that these authorities have a proper understanding of beneficial ownership requirements and comply with the FATF's requirements for holding this information because they may be more familiar with how beneficial ownership information is used in the context of their own work (for example, tax authorities might be more familiar with exchange of information for tax purposes and not the FATF standards). In addition, fiscal confidentiality rules that tax authorities may otherwise be subject to should not apply to beneficial ownership information.

Alternatively, the registry could be held by a private body that a public authority entrusts to do so, such as businesses or business associations that may already be involved in the creation of legal persons (for example, a Chamber of

Commerce, notary association). The use of such private sector entities will require some form of oversight at the government level to ensure that tasks are performed effectively and in compliance with the relevant AML/CFT requirements, and clear criteria for competent authorities' access and use of the information will need to be developed (as with government-run registries).

Key Considerations

Types of legal persons. In general, a registry should cover companies and other types of legal persons created in a country. Where a country adopts a decentralized registry approach (for example, in federal systems or between sectors), efforts should be made to ensure that all relevant legal persons are still covered, based on the risk assessment.

A country may consider that certain types of legal entities do not need to provide beneficial ownership information to the register; for example, companies listed on a stock exchange may not need to register if they are already subject to stringent disclosure and transparency requirements.[2] Another example is state-owned enterprises that are ultimately owned by the public and managed by the state (or state functionaries) as a fiduciary in the public interest. The concept of beneficial ownership in its traditional sense in the AML/CFT frameworks does not apply to state-owned enterprises. However, transparency of ownership and control is nevertheless critical for their effective functioning and for the detection of corruption, conflict of interest, or any rent-seeking behavior by their management. OECD (2015) prescribes as best practice the disclosure of governance, ownership, and voting structure of the entity, and civil society groups have also called for governments to include information on the ownership structure of state-owned enterprises in their beneficial ownership reporting requirements.[3] In such cases, these entities can be included in the registry with a note that no beneficial ownership information is available or applies to them and where information on their ownership and/or control structures can otherwise be found. Countries should be able to provide clear reasoning based on their risk understanding if they do allow for any such related exemptions.

Based on the risk assessment, countries may choose which foreign legal persons with high money laundering or terrorist financing risks and a sufficient link to the country are required to also provide information to the registry on their beneficial owner. This can be a requirement imposed on the foreign legal person before they are permitted to operate in the country.

---

[2] FATF Recommendation 10 makes it clear that for the purpose of customer due diligence (CDD)— where the customer or the owner of the controlling interest is a company listed on a stock exchange (and subject to disclosure requirements either by stock exchange rules or through law or other enforceable means) that imposes requirements to ensure adequate transparency of beneficial ownership, or is a majority-owned subsidiary of such a company—it is not necessary to identify and verify the identity of any shareholder or beneficial owner of such companies. The relevant identification data may be obtained from a public register, from the customer, or from other reliable sources. The same reasoning should apply in relation to the registry.

[3] See, for example, Lord (2021); OECD (2018, Chapter 2; 2021); Open Ownership (January 2021); Open Ownership (2021a).

Data collection and verification. The type of information that a registry can collect will depend partly on what is needed to ensure that the information is accurate, adequate, and up to date. An authority/body running a database or registry should have the legal structure, resources (technical, financial, and human), and legal powers to request and obtain the information, including additional information as required for enhanced verification. To support verification processes, it would also help to hold these data in a machine-readable format.

Where countries have a system that has several interlinked registries/databases (for example, in federal systems or between sectors), it is important that the different registries comply with the same standards—including the same definition of beneficial ownership—and that they carry out verification checks to avoid regulatory arbitrage. Additionally, a variety of other information sources can provide insights into beneficial ownership information (for example, property registers, bank registers). Consideration should be given to allow the public authority/body responsible for the registry to have access to this information to help with additional verification checks.

Timeliness of updates. Countries should clearly set out the timing of filing and updating information in a registry, and the registry should have relevant powers to enforce these requirements. Legal persons or others who provide information to the registry (such as TCSPs, in systems where TCSPs have responsibility for obtaining beneficial ownership information) must be provided with a legally binding time frame (about a month or sooner) to produce or update this information or face dissuasive sanctions for not doing so. To the extent possible, updates to information should be done in real time, and the registry should maintain historical records of changes in beneficial ownership.

Dissuasive sanctions. The operator of the register should have the power to impose penalties if this information is not provided or is inaccurate, and actually impose them in such cases. These should be sufficiently dissuasive so that they are not perceived as a cost of doing business. Penalties that can be imposed include administrative sanctions and criminal penalties against individuals (including the beneficial owner or officers of the company) or the legal person. These can include dissuasive monetary sanctions, making an individual criminally liable for failure to provide the information or providing inaccurate information, not permitting registration or incorporation of a legal person, or striking a legal person from a register.

The power to remove an existing legal person from the registry is a sanction that is typically available even where legal persons do not provide basic information to a company registry. However, this tends to be poorly enforced, even by company registries. Authorities should consider extending this sanction where legal persons fail to provide beneficial ownership or provide inaccurate information. Authorities should also consider publicly disclosing the reasons for the legal person to be removed from the register, that is, to issue a notice that the legal person failed to comply with the requirements for beneficial ownership information and, as a result, was removed from the register. Consideration should also be given to barring directors and managers of companies from operating other legal persons when they are found to have provided inaccurate beneficial ownership information or committed other relevant acts.

Sanctions should also extend to notaries and TCSPs and the like if they are responsible for submitting/updating beneficial ownership information in a register, including making them criminally liable if they are found to have purposefully or negligently provided inaccurate or misleading information.

Access to information, including tiered and public access. Public registries of beneficial ownership information, which already exist in some countries, have some important benefits compared with closed registries. It allows other competent authorities, the private sector, and interested parties (for example, civil society) to check legal and beneficial ownership information, which can reduce costs and burdens on other parts of the system. Public registers also simplify both domestic and cross-border information exchange and cooperation. For instance, if foreign competent authorities can directly access information in a public database, it can reduce the need for formal information exchange requests. Similarly, if a domestic competent authority has direct access to a central register, then there is no need to engage in information exchange upon request, which will save time and resources.

To address data privacy concerns, consideration should be given to offering tiered access to relevant stakeholders. For example, the general public might be given access to the name and country of residence of a beneficial owner. Financial institutions and DNFBPs, which are required to perform CDD obligations as well as any discrepancy reporting duties, may additionally be given access to the type of information that they would normally have to ask of customers (for example, date of birth, address). Competent authorities should be given direct and instant access to the full set of information held by the registry when they need it to carry out their normal duties (for example, supervisory authorities engaged in licensing, tax authorities issuing tax identification numbers) or when authorized to do so (for example, investigative bodies as part of a criminal investigation).

To determine which information should be made available to the public or should be restricted, countries could adhere to need-to-know principles and/or have opt-out principles (certain information will not be disclosed because of data privacy, identity theft, or other risk considerations). These considerations will vary from country to country.[4] That said, even in such cases, law enforcement should continue to have full access to the information in the registry. The FATF standards encourage countries to consider facilitating public access to this information.

If a country chooses to hold beneficial ownership information in multiple registries rather than one central registry (for example, in a federal system), its effectiveness and usefulness might be affected negatively if these databases lack a central access point. Having beneficial ownership information held in different systems can also increase the burden on financial institutions and DNFBPs and others who may need to check these registries for information. Therefore, it is

---

[4] An example is the European Union's 4th and 5th Money Laundering Directives, which mandate public registries of beneficial ownership information except where the beneficial owner might be open "to disproportionate risk, risk of fraud, kidnapping, blackmail, extortion, harassment, violence, or intimidation, or where the beneficial owner is a minor or otherwise legally incapable, Member States may provide for an exemption from such access to all or part of the information on the beneficial ownership on a case-by-case basis" (Directive [EU] 2018/843, Article 30, para. 9).

important to ensure that in such a decentralized system, efforts are made to inter-link the different registries where data are held and ensure that these data are in the same format (for ease of comparison). If they are not interlinked, a country should allow all its registries to be searched at the same time.

Discrepancy reporting. Regardless of whether a country chooses to adopt a public database or a closed database, consideration should be given to extending access to the information in this registry to reporting entities, including FIs and DNFBPs. This can help with verifying information in the registry but also help reporting entities in carrying out their own CDD obligations. For this to be effective, countries should strongly consider introducing legal or administrative requirements for discrepancy reporting. For the reporting entity, such findings could also be considered a potential red flag that can support filing suspicious transaction information. Countries could also consider extending such discrepancy reporting requirements to competent authorities that have access to beneficial ownership information through their core work. In addition, civil society organizations and the general public could also be allowed to report discrepancies noted in public registries.

Resource implications. Depending on their forms, registries can be costly to set up and maintain. Their most basic function is to provide a mechanism for the authorities (and other relevant stakeholders or the public) to keep track of legal persons. Beyond updating the legal framework and finding resources, the public authority or body must be able to have systems (for example, information technology systems) in place to receive beneficial ownership information and to maintain and update them. In addition, training on beneficial ownership must be provided to a potentially large number of staff to understand relevant tax, company, and AML/CFT laws and to recognize potential abuse (for example, red flags), especially because the registry will also have a verification role.

In particular, creating databases to collect and hold beneficial ownership information from scratch can take a considerable amount of time. For databases working with paper files, this means clearing backlogs, removing defunct legal persons, and implementing some form of automation/digitalization as a priority. Nevertheless, ongoing technological developments can help drive down the cost of establishing and maintaining registries. In addition, any cost-benefit analysis of registries should also consider the long-term benefits of registries, for example, to reduce costs associated with investigations and responding to international cooperation requests.[5]

Some countries have implemented a fee structure to provide access to information from a register. This can help generate the necessary resources and financing to run the registry. However, it is important to ensure that the fee structure imposed does not inhibit the broader objective of transparency. Competent authorities and those that need to check the register (for example, banks) should always be able to access it without payment, and for other interested parties, consideration should be given to imposing a reasonable/nominal fee to allow them to search the registry (for example, countries should avoid requiring a

---

[5] In 2002, HM Treasury in the United Kingdom carried out an impact analysis which estimated that the disclosure of beneficial ownership information by unlisted companies through a public register of beneficial ownership could yield savings (in time and resources) to UK law enforcement.

payment for each search entry). See further discussion in Chapter 5, "Policy Considerations and Regulatory Impact."

Role of technology. Technological advances such as interoperable data standards and blockchain can support measures to verify and enhance the accuracy and timeliness of beneficial ownership information. A number of emerging initiatives are promising in this respect (see Box 3.3). See Guiding Questions for Registry Approach (Box 3.4).

Box 3.3. The Role of Technology in Improving the Implementation and Accuracy of Beneficial Ownership Registers

To effectively verify the accuracy of information in beneficial ownership registers and increase its effectiveness, the data contained in them should be interoperable with data from both domestic and international sources. Given the volume of data such registers process, an effective verification system should be at least partly automated, requiring the data to be in an open data format. To address this challenge, a working group made up of anti–money laundering, anti-corruption, and transparency civil society organizations established the Beneficial Ownership Data Standard, a framework for collecting and presenting beneficial ownership data in a standardized and interoperable format (Open Ownership, n.d.). Its schema facilitates comparison of beneficial ownership data with other domestic sources of data (such as property registers) and enables timely sharing of information with competent authorities in foreign jurisdictions. The structured data collection process proposed in the standard can also help provide precise natural and legal person identifiers, offering greater confidence to the ultimate data users.

Some countries that already operate beneficial ownership registers have turned to technology to address some of the verification and accuracy challenges with the data collected to date. For example, in one country, upon registration of a new legal person, the registry automatically cross-checks the business address provided against the country's address register to verify that it is a genuine address within the country (FATF 2019).

More recently, there has also been a push to establish greater interoperability between these registries. Under the European Union's 5th Anti–Money Laundering Directive, released in 2018, member states' beneficial ownership registers should be interconnected under the European Central Platform to facilitate cooperation and investigations across jurisdictions (Directive [EU] 2018/843).

Academic researchers have also begun exploring the possibility of blockchain technologies providing near-real-time updates and exchanges of beneficial ownership information. Current beneficial ownership registers offer a snapshot of a legal person's beneficial ownership declared at a specific point in time, but the ability to accurately reflect changes in beneficial ownership often relies on legal persons providing updated information to the registry (de Jong, Meyer, and Owens 2017). Blockchain's distributed ledger technologies offer the possibility of beneficial ownership information being updated in near real time. This technology can also better track changes in ownership over time, enabling the identification of red flags in the historical patterns of beneficial ownership of a legal person. Distributed ledger technology removes the risk of data tampering at a central point of failure, such as a central beneficial ownership database (Vaidyanathan, Mathur, and Modak 2018).

Box 3.4. Guiding Questions: Registry Approach

Type of Register

- Is there a register with beneficial ownership information on legal persons?
  - Is it a stand-alone register, or is it set up as part of another register (for example, a beneficial ownership register as part of the country's central register of all legal persons, or a beneficial ownership register kept by private sector bodies involved in the creation of legal persons [professional bodies representing notaries, trust and company service providers])?
  - Does the register cover all legal persons or industry-specific legal persons (for example, extractive companies, companies engaged in procurement)?
  - What is the legal basis for the beneficial ownership register?
  - Which authority/agency is responsible for the management of the beneficial ownership register?
  - Does this authority/agency have sufficient powers and adequate resources to take on this responsibility?
    - Financial resources to ensure adequate maintenance of the information technology infrastructure?
    - Human resources to ensure that information in the register remains accurate and up to date?
    - Are these human resources adequately trained on the concept of beneficial ownership and transparency of legal persons, more generally?
    - Are there any government oversight measures to ensure effective implementation if the register is kept and managed by private sector bodies?

Required Data

- What type of data are included in the register (for example, details on the legal person, personal data, chain of ownership)?
  - Does it extend to foreign legal persons with a sufficient link in the country?
  - Is a distinction made for sensitive data?
- How are data entered in the register?
  - Online by representatives of the legal person or gatekeepers involved in the creation and management of the legal person?
  - Manually by staff of the authority/agency in charge of the register?
  - What type of supporting documents should be provided (for example, proof of incorporation, passport or other identity document or national identification number for each of the beneficial owners)?
    - Are there specific measures to verify the identity of the beneficial owner being provided to the register and to verify the information submitted?
    - Are there specific measures in place to ensure reliability of these supporting documents when ownership and management are entirely nonresident?
- Is the data entered into the register in an open data format (for example, the Beneficial Ownership Data Standard)?

Verification and Discrepancy Reporting

- What measures are in place to verify, monitor, and ensure that data in the register are/remain adequate, accurate, and up to date?
  - At the time of creation of the legal person and at a later stage when changes occur?

(Continued)

Box 3.4. Continued

- How is verification carried out? What documents are required for verification?
- Is a risk-based approach applied to verification of information?
- Are there any specific measures in place to identify nominees and/or strawmen?
- Are nominee shareholders and directors required to disclose their nominee status and the identity of their nominator in the registry?
- How often and how quickly should beneficial ownership information in the register be updated when changes occur?
- Are legal persons/registered agents required by law to update beneficial ownership information in the register when changes occur? What is the time frame for providing updated information (for example, within 30 days of the change occurring)?
- Are competent authorities and/or other entities using the register required to report discrepancies between the beneficial ownership information in the register and the beneficial ownership information in their records to the authority/agency in charge of the central register?
  - Does any guidance exist to report discrepancies?
  - Are stakeholders trained to take on this important role?
  - What enforcement mechanisms or penalties are imposed on entities using the register for failing to report discrepancies?
- What is the process for reporting these discrepancies, including timing of the reporting?

Penalties

- What actions are taken when no or incorrect beneficial ownership information is filed and/or changes in beneficial ownership are not reported?
  - Actions when no beneficial ownership information has been filed?
  - Actions when changes in beneficial ownership have not been reported?
- What actions are taken when beneficial ownership information filed is false?
- What sanctioning measures are taken for failure to file (updates to) or submission of false beneficial ownership information?
  - How is it ensured that failures are addressed following a sanction?

Access to Information

- How will this information be accessed? Online? Is a hard copy of the register available?
- Who has access to the information?
- What information can be accessed?
  - Are there any limitations to access by competent authorities?
  - Are there any limitations to access by obliged entities?
  - Are there any limitations to access by public authorities in the course of public procurement?
  - Are there any limitations/special requirements related to access by the general public?
- Are there any requirements for accessing the data?
  - Are potential users of the data required to pay a fee to access the data?
  - Are potential users of the data required to register or provide any form of identification to access the data?
- Is there any guidance to obliged entities on their access to the beneficial ownership register and the use of the information?
- How quickly can the information be accessed?

Additional Supplementary Measures—Information Held by Financial Institutions and DNFBPs

> *Weaknesses in CDD measures have an impact on the ability of financial institutions and DNFBPs to hold adequate, accurate, and up-to-date beneficial ownership information.*

Overview

The FATF recommendations (for example, FATF Recommendations 8, 10, 12, 16, and 22) require financial institutions and DNFBPs, as part of their CDD measures, to identify and verify the beneficial ownership of their clients who are legal persons.[6] Financial institutions such as banks will often have legal persons as clients. DNFBPs might act for legal persons, such as real estate agents acting for legal persons who are buying or selling real estate and thus will need to know who is the beneficial owner. TCSPs, accountants, and lawyers or notaries often act on behalf of legal person clients and/or are involved in the creation of legal persons and thus need to understand their beneficial ownership if they are carrying out one of the activities covered by the FATF recommendations.[7]

In some jurisdictions, TCSPs often have initial and ongoing contact with legal persons, which can be of assistance when keeping track of beneficial ownership. They can be involved in creating a legal person but also in providing ongoing services, such as acting as nominee directors or shareholders or offering company secretarial services. In some countries, it is compulsory to use a TCSP when forming a legal person, whereas their use is optional in others. In other countries, these roles are often taken by the legal or accounting sectors acting in their traditional capacity. TCSPs can vary in size and complexity, often with many small players operating on behalf of domestic and international clients. As such, the quality of compliance with AML/CFT requirements can vary greatly.

Notarial models generally entail an attestation of registry filings by a notary who is a public employee directly responsible to a government ministry, or a legal professional entrusted by law to perform certain tasks for these filings to take legal effect. In this model, notaries are obliged to identify and maintain beneficial ownership information. They are required to collect information pertaining to all parties involved in an activity or transaction, including the beneficial owner. Such a model requires proper resourcing and an appropriate legal structure (including penalties for notaries who fail to collect that information and for legal persons

---

[6] DNFBP, in FATF terms, refers to casinos, real estate agents, dealers in precious metals and stones, lawyers, notaries and accountants, and trust and company service providers. The FATF recommendations do not cover all activities for each of these sectors, but for trust and company service providers, acting as a formation agent of legal persons is covered, as are other services to legal persons (see FATF Glossary).

[7] For example, the FATF recommendations require that CDD and other requirements apply to lawyers and notaries if they are engaged in creating, operating, or management of legal persons.

providing incorrect information) to ensure that the information is accurate. Furthermore, for such a system to work, the risk and context of each country must be evaluated, including the sector's level of integrity.

Therefore, to clarify, financial institutions and DNFBPs can have two distinct roles that should not be confused. They may have a role in company creation—in general, this relates to DNFBPs such as TCSPs or notaries. However, financial institutions and DNFBPs also have regular CDD obligations—which include obtaining beneficial ownership information—when doing business with a legal person.

Key Considerations

Financial institutions and DNFBPs can be a good source of beneficial ownership information. However, there are some limitations that must be mitigated for them to be effective sources of information. The lack of effective implementation of even basic CDD measures by financial institutions and DNFBPs in many countries is a potential challenge. If financial institutions and DNFBPs are not effectively implementing basic CDD measures, then it is likely to be very difficult to ensure that they are willing or able to effectively implement the more elaborate beneficial ownership requirements.

In addition, financial institutions and DNFBPs can also face challenges with identifying and verifying beneficial ownership information, including a lack of capacity and resources. Investments are needed up front, including to train staff to understand the concept of beneficial ownership and identify circumstances where it is not being provided or is being provided in a way that might be suspicious. One of the common challenges that financial institutions and DNFBPs face is to what level they should search for a beneficial owner and the proof they require to establish that a natural person is a beneficial owner. Nevertheless, as part of regular onboarding of new customers, financial institutions and DNFBPs should have a good understanding of the customer's business profile and structure, which is useful information to identify and verify the beneficial owner.

The international standards technically allow financial institutions and DNFBPs to list the identity of the senior managing official if there is either doubt that the controlling legal owner is the beneficial owner or that no natural person exerts control through ownership interests. However, this should be permitted only in very exceptional circumstances (for example, it could be considered when dealing with very large public or multinational corporations where the ownership structures of such companies are highly diversified but also well known). If no natural person is identified as beneficial owner, the natural person identified as a senior managing official should be recorded and identified as holding this position, and not identified as the beneficial owner. In all other instances, there should be little to no excuse as to why a financial institution or DNFBP cannot identify the beneficial owner. Given that companies are expected to know their beneficial owners (under the revised FATF standards), there should be little reason for them to not share this information with the financial institution or DNFBP or other competent authorities. If companies are unwilling to share this information, then this would be a red flag for the financial institution or DNFBP. Furthermore, under the FATF standards, financial institutions and DNFBPs are required to not open accounts, commence business relationships, or perform transactions or terminate business relationships if they are unable to comply with relevant CDD measures.

This discrepancy has also been recognized in the context of the March 2022 changes to the FATF's definition of beneficial ownership, which now clarifies that this provision of Recommendation 10 does not amend or supersede the definition of who is the beneficial owner but only sets out how CDD should be conducted in situations where the beneficial owner cannot be identified. In this regard, countries should ensure that existing definitions of beneficial ownership in their relevant laws reflect this accurately and make relevant amendments if they drafted these definitions based on the FATF Recommendation 10 test for beneficial ownership.

In addition, even if accurate beneficial ownership information has been obtained at the start of the customer relationship, if the legal person's risk and business profile does not change, or as long as the legal person does not obtain new products or services, the financial institution or DNFBP may not be aware of any changes to the legal person's beneficial ownership information unless changes are communicated to the financial institution or DNFBP. Although this has a limited impact on the CDD of the bank, it has a negative impact on the usefulness for other purposes of beneficial ownership information obtained and held by financial institutions or DNFBPs. Financial institutions and DNFBPs should have processes in place to ensure that beneficial ownership information they hold for their customers remains up to date as part of their ongoing customer relationship monitoring (for example, by requiring the relevant customer to file know-your-customer documents regularly).

It is highly recommended that, if TCSPs or other gatekeepers (notaries, lawyers, accountants) are responsible for setting up legal persons, they should be required to maintain records of the beneficial ownership information that they collect through their role in company formation and for their CDD purposes. This information should be maintained in the country of incorporation. In some cases, the gatekeeper might also be responsible for providing beneficial ownership information directly to the public authority or body that will hold this information.

Competent authorities such as supervisors should set out clear expectations as to what is required of gatekeepers and take steps via the supervisory process to ensure that identification and verification of beneficial ownership information is happening in practice. A system relying on collection and verification of beneficial ownership by TCSPs, lawyers, accountants, or notaries is more likely to be effective in a country where the authorities properly supervise and oversee such DNFBPs and where the DNFBPs tend to act with integrity. But such a system will not be as reliable in countries where these sectors are more susceptible to corruption (see further discussion in this chapter's "Supervision and Monitoring" section).

The information that financial institutions and DNFBPs collect may not necessarily or immediately be available to third parties, including to competent authorities. The revised FATF standards require that countries should be able to determine in a timely manner whether a company has or controls an account with a financial institution within a country. To do this, countries should consider having centralized or interconnected bank account registries that competent authorities can check to determine if a legal person is a client of one or more financial institutions as one way to ensure that countries have timely access to this information.

Once financial institutions and DNFBPs collect beneficial ownership information, this could become information that is potentially subject to financial secrecy and data protection provisions. Depending on a country's legal system, competent authorities may need different legal powers to obtain information (for example, court orders or warrants). In countries where TCSPs and other gatekeepers play a role in the creation, registration, or incorporation of legal persons, access to beneficial ownership information may be affected by claims of legal or professional privilege. Countries using such systems should have clear rules that legal or professional privilege does not apply with respect to beneficial ownership information (see Box 3.5). See Guiding Questions for Financial Institutions and DNFBPs (Box 3.6).

Box 3.5. Legal Professional Privilege or Professional Secrecy

Access to beneficial ownership information held by a lawyer, notary, accountant, or trust and company service provider should never be subject to legal professional privilege or professional secrecy.

It is important to note that there is a wide variation between countries in their understanding of the scope of legal professional privilege. In general, the principle of legal professional privilege/secrecy protects communications between legal professionals and their clients, treating them as confidential. Information subject to such privilege is usually exempted from disclosure in investigative or legal proceedings to encourage free and full disclosure in such relationships, without fear of subsequent disclosure.

This right is conferred upon the client, who can consent to its waiver, or the information could be disclosed in certain limited circumstances—for example, when the legal professional is being used to perpetrate a crime. In addition, the scope of the privilege generally does not extend to communications pertaining to commercial advice or fiduciary services and to beneficial ownership information obtained thereby.

That said, legal professional privilege continues to pose obstacles and challenges for law enforcement agencies in obtaining beneficial ownership information from legal professional service providers. The client may claim privilege and initiate judicial proceedings to protect the information from disclosure, including if they have been tipped off by their attorneys in the context of ongoing investigations. Furthermore, legal professional service providers may themselves lack adequate knowledge of the scope of the privilege or may fear disciplinary action or litigation proceedings because of incorrect application of the privilege, prompting them to take an expansive approach and invoke it. This poses additional hurdles and challenges in accessing beneficial ownership information because law enforcement may need to overcome court proceedings to obtain the information, which may also result in delays. In the case of a complex, multijurisdictional legal structure, legal professionals from many different countries could be involved, thereby posing similar challenges in obtaining beneficial ownership information from that jurisdiction's legal professional services provider.

This issue has been discussed in detail by the FATF (2013b).

Sources: FATF 2013b; and IMF staff.

Box 3.6. Guiding Questions: Financial Institutions and DNFBPs

- Are there adequate measures in place requiring reporting entities to take reasonable measures to understand the ownership and control structure of a legal person and to identify beneficial owners and verify their identity?
  - What is the relevant legal basis?
  - Do the same measures apply to both financial institutions and designated nonfinancial businesses and professions (DNFBPs), or are there differences?
  - Are there certain categories of financial institutions and/or DNFBPs that are not subject to beneficial ownership requirements?
- Is there adequate guidance for financial institutions and DNFBPs on the implementation of beneficial ownership requirements?
  - Does the guidance include a definition of beneficial ownership consistent with the FATF requirements and include concepts of both ownership and control?
  - Does the guidance focus on ensuring that beneficial ownership information remains accurate and up to date?
  - Does the guidance contain details on understanding the ownership and control structure of a legal person?
    - Do any thresholds apply?
    - Does it differentiate between domestic and foreign ownership?
  - Do financial institutions and DNFBPs receive training to enhance their understanding of the concept of beneficial ownership and what is expected from them in terms of identification of beneficial ownership?
- Is implementation of beneficial ownership requirements assessed as part of anti–money laundering and combating the financing of terrorism (AML/CFT) supervision?
  - Are all categories of financial institutions and DNFBPs supervised for AML/CFT purposes?
  - Is the implementation of beneficial ownership requirements part of off-site monitoring or on-site or targeted supervision?
  - Regarding beneficial ownership information, are checks in place to verify that financial institutions and DNFBPs hold accurate and up-to-date information on beneficial ownerships?
- Do all competent authorities have adequate powers to sanction noncompliance with AML/CFT obligations, including beneficial ownership requirements?
  - Which supervisors do not have (adequate) sanctioning powers?
  - Are sanctions effective, proportionate, and dissuasive?
- What measures are in place to ensure that deficiencies are addressed following sanctions?
  - Do competent authorities have powers to obtain timely access to beneficial ownership information kept by financial institutions and DNFBPs?
  - Do these powers extend to all types of financial institutions and DNFBPs? Are there any exceptions (that is, professions that invoke legal privilege)?
  - Do certain conditions apply to such access (for example, court orders, search warrants)?
  - How quickly can the information be obtained from financial institutions and DNFBPs?
  - What measures are in place to inform supervisors of deficiencies in
    - Making beneficial ownership information available to competent authorities?
    - The scope of beneficial ownership information maintained by obliged entities?
- Do financial institutions and DNFBPs have access to beneficial ownership information if this is held by a public authority/body, and are there requirements for discrepancy reporting?

THE LIFE CYCLE OF A LEGAL PERSON

The ownership and control of a legal person may change during its life cycle. Beneficial ownership will need to be collected at various stages between the creation of a legal person to its ultimate dissolution.

A legal person is likely to go through several stages in its existence. Each stage will have implications for the way beneficial ownership is obtained, held, and made available to competent authorities in a timely manner. Different stakeholders might hold beneficial ownership information at different stages of a legal person's life cycle (for example, at creation, a company registry or a gatekeeper may collect this information, and it would also be collected when the legal person becomes a client of a financial institution or DNFBP).

The following sections will set out the various stages in the life of a legal person and the environment in which it has to operate, and suggest measures that should be considered at each of these stages to ensure the availability of adequate, accurate, and up-to-date basic and beneficial ownership information pertaining to the legal person. This chapter considers what information needs to be collected during the various stages (see Figure 3.3), as follows:

- *Creation and registration.* What type of basic and beneficial ownership information should be collected at these stages and what steps need to be taken to verify that this information is accurate;

- *Interactions of legal persons.* What information a legal person needs to provide during its existence, for example, in the context of CDD measures and sharing information with other competent authorities;

- *Changes to the legal person.* How and when to update this information, including changes further up the chain of ownership;

- *Supervision/enforcement.* How to ensure the accuracy and availability of beneficial information at all stages of a legal person's life, including in the context of monitoring/supervision and wider enforcement actions taken against the legal person; and

- *Liquidation/dissolution.* The record-keeping requirements for beneficial ownership information when a legal person is dissolved.

Figure 3.3. Beneficial Ownership Information during the Life Cycle of a Legal Person

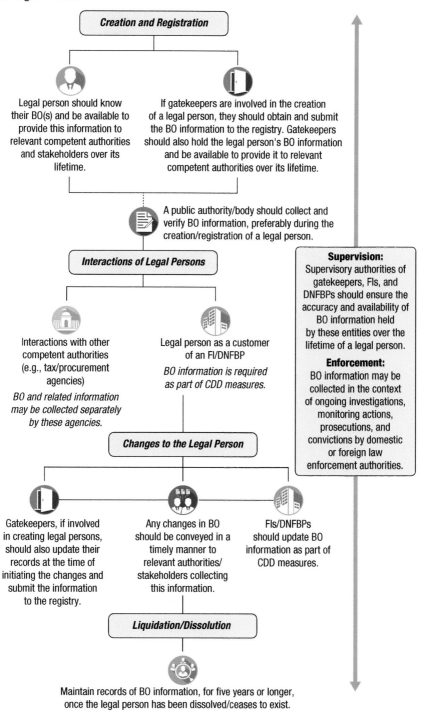

Sources: Financial Action Task Force; and IMF staff.
Note: BO = beneficial ownership; CDD = customer due diligence; DNFBP = designated nonfinancial businesses and professions; FI = financial institution.

Creation and Registration

Different types of documents should be collected with respect to basic and beneficial ownership information to prove the identity of natural persons and their means and mechanisms of control over the legal person.

Legal persons can be created in several different ways, depending on the country's legal framework.[8] Entities can be created in person, by registration with a company registry, by gatekeepers such as notaries and TCSPs, online, or a combination of each. The ways these entities can be formed will determine at which stages information should be collected and who should verify this information.

A certain amount of basic/legal and beneficial ownership information should be collected at the creation and/or registration stage. Countries generally have mechanisms to enable them to collect the minimum amount of basic information for the authorities to be comfortable that a legal person is allowed to operate there. In general, beneficial ownership information should also be collected along with basic information rather than trying to collect this information after a legal person has been created. Collecting beneficial ownership information along with the existing basic information at creation and registration should be done efficiently to enable countries to offer an attractive business environment. Countries could also consider strengthening the requirements for beneficial ownership information by requiring that companies cannot be incorporated until beneficial ownership information is registered with the relevant public authority/body or an alternative mechanism, as is the case for basic information.

Basic or Legal Information to Be Collected at Creation and Registration

The following is the minimum basic information on legal persons that countries are required to collect:

- Company name;
- Proof of incorporation;
- Legal form and status;
- Address of the registered office;
- Basic regulating powers (for example, for companies, the memorandum and articles of association for companies and for other legal persons, laws, founding documents, bylaws, deeds);
- List of directors; and
- Unique identifier such as a tax identification number or equivalent (where this exists).

The legal person should obtain and record this information. It should also be recorded in a company registry and be publicly available.

---

[8] Any reference to "company" in this section should be taken as requiring similar measures for any other forms of legal persons, consistent with the FATF standards.

In addition, legal persons are required to maintain a register of their shareholders or members. The company should keep this information within the country at its registered office or at another location notified to the company registry (for example, with a third party under the company's responsibility). This register should contain the number of shares held by each shareholder and categories of shares (including the nature of the associated voting rights).

Note that the FATF standards allow that, if the legal person or the relevant company registry also holds beneficial ownership information within the country, then the register of shareholders does not necessarily have to be in the country if the legal persons can provide this information promptly on request. This is because in most cases, the same shareholders will also be the beneficial owners. What is important is to ensure that competent authorities can access beneficial ownership information promptly within the country.

In addition to the regular basic and legal information that the international standards require, some countries also collect additional information (for example, a legal person identifier where one exists, legal and trading addresses, names of all senior managers, and the like).[9]

See Guiding Questions for Basic Information (Box 3.7).

Box 3.7. Guiding Questions: Basic Information

Company Registry

- Is it required by law or other enforceable means that the relevant authority should collect *at a minimum* the basic information at the time of creation and incorporation of the legal person?
    - Which law or laws at the federal, state, or provincial level?
    - What type of supporting documents are requested to verify basic information (for example, passport or national identity document, national identification number [issued by social security system, tax, or other relevant authorities])?

Information to Be Recorded by Company Registry

- Is there one central registry at the federal level, or are there various registries at the state and/or provincial level?
- What is the legal basis for the central/decentralized registry/registries?
    - Which authorities/agencies are responsible for managing the central/various registry/registries?
    - Do the authorities/agencies have adequate resources to take on this responsibility?
- How are data on basic information entered in the registry/registries?
    - What additional measures, if any, are put in place to ensure that recording is accurate?

(Continued)

---

[9] An example is the Legal Entity Identifier by the Global LEI Foundation, which has rolled out a 20-character, alpha-numeric code that connects to reference information that enables identification of legal entities.

Box 3.7. Continued

- What type of documents should be provided to support data submission?
- Are there specific measures in place to ensure the reliability of these supporting documents when ownership and management are entirely nonresident?
- Does the register record all the requisite basic information, namely:
  - Company name;
  - Proof of incorporation (for example, date of certificate of incorporation);
  - Legal form and status (for example, limited liability, limited by guarantee);
  - Address of registered office;
  - Basic regulating powers (for example, Articles of Association);
  - List of directors, including directors who are both natural and legal persons; and
  - Unique identifier such as a tax identification number or equivalent (where this exists).

Publicly Available Information

- Is it required by law that basic information should be publicly available?
- How can the information be accessed?
  - Directly through one or more (central/decentralized) registries or online platforms by external service providers?
    - Is access free of charge? If not, what are the costs associated with this access?
    - Is access unlimited, or are there any restrictions on access?
- In what language or languages is the information available? Is there a possibility to add a name in any language/script?

Information Held by Companies

- Is there a requirement for companies to maintain information in law or other enforceable means?
- Is there guidance for companies on the implementation of this requirement?
- Is the information maintained within the country at a location notified to the company registry?
- Which authority/agency monitors the implementation of this requirement?
- Does the authority/agency have the necessary powers to impose sanctions in case of breaches of this requirement?

Register of Shareholders or Members

- Is the register kept within the country?
- Who holds the register?
  - The company at its registered office?
  - The company at another location notified to the registry?
  - A third person designated by the company at a location notified to the registry?
    - If a third person, what is the relationship with the company?
    - If a third person, is it an obliged entity subject to anti–money laundering and combating the financing of terrorism requirements?
    - Is there a record of the number of shares held by each shareholder? What are the categories of shares (for example, ordinary shares, redeemable shares, preference shares)? What is the nature of voting rights (for example, one vote per share, one vote per shareholder, golden shares [with higher voting rights])?
    - In cases of nominee shareholders and directors, is their nominee status and identity of their nominator included in the company register?

Beneficial Ownership Information to Be Collected at Creation and Registration/Incorporation: Identification and Verification

The FATF standards do not contain a set list of required documentation that countries should collect to establish beneficial ownership. Although the FATF standards set out clearly what basic information needs to be collected, the type of beneficial ownership information to be collected can vary and should be result oriented (that is, it will vary depending on the type of legal person and what is required to reasonably verify the beneficial owner of that particular legal person). In some instances, the basic information collected will be sufficient to identify the beneficial owner. To the extent required, information collected on the beneficial owner should include information on their identity and their means and mechanisms of control. See Box 3.8 for examples of the type of information that can be collected.[10]

Box 3.8. Identification of Beneficial Owner

Identity of a Beneficial Owner

Once the name of a beneficial owner has been provided, their identity should be validated. This includes checking to a reasonable extent that the natural person is who they claim to be. The information that could be taken to confirm this includes:

- Valid government-issued identity card;
- Valid government-issued passport;
- Driving license;
- Information from a government source or embassy confirming identity; and
- Reliable e-identity software.

This should be supported by credible publicly available information.

Means and Mechanisms of Ownership and Control

In addition, information should be collected on why the natural person is the beneficial owner, such as:

- An extract of a shareholder registry showing ownership;
- Any nominee agreement that shows who exercises real control behind a shareholder arrangement;
- A shareholders' agreement that shows a natural person is able to control the shares of more than one shareholder, effectively giving control;
- Documentary evidence that the natural person is able to exercise a dominant influence over the legal person;
- Documentary evidence that the natural person has the power to appoint senior management; and
- Documentary evidence (for example, an employment contract) that a director or employee is able to influence the legal person.

---

[10] See also Open Ownership (n.d.) for examples of the type of information that can be collected. The Beneficial Ownership Data Standard is an attempt to standardize data collection in relation to beneficial ownership information by a working group of public, private, and civil society stakeholders.

Day-to-Day Interactions by a Legal Person

A legal person will likely have ongoing business relationships with financial institutions and DNFBPs during its existence and must provide beneficial ownership information to them as part of CDD requirements, in addition to the requirement to take certain steps when it is formed. Furthermore, the legal person might be required to provide beneficial ownership or related information to other authorities (for example, tax authorities, procurement authorities) in the context of other activities and interactions they may have. Legal persons may also change their beneficial owners over the course of these relationships/interactions, and this can influence where and how beneficial ownership should be obtained and held.

Relationship with Financial Institutions and DNFBPs

> *Where financial institutions and DNFBPs rely on third parties to conduct CDD, they should be able to easily access beneficial ownership information they hold. Financial institutions and DNFBPs should also have effective risk management systems to determine whether a beneficial owner is a PEP or a family member or close associate of one.*

The requirements on financial institutions and DNFBPs and the challenges they face are set out in Chapter 3, "Additional Supplementary Measures—Information Held by Financial Institutions and DNFBPs." Additionally, legal persons should be required to cooperate with requests for information in relation to beneficial ownership from financial institutions and DNFBPs. Failure to do so can ultimately lead to the financial institution or DNFBP submitting a suspicious transaction report on the legal person, putting accounts on hold, and/or terminating a business relationship.

Financial institutions and DNFBPs are also required to consider beneficial ownership in the wider context of carrying out CDD, namely in relation to third-party reliance and when taking steps to identify customers who might be PEPs or the family and close associates of a PEP. If financial institutions and DNFBPs are allowed to rely on third parties to carry out certain CDD functions, including identification of the beneficial owner of a customer, additional requirements apply. These include making sure that the information about, inter alia, the identity of the beneficial owner is obtained immediately and ensuring that copies of identification data will be made available on request. Countries should ensure that where they permit third-party reliance, there are provisions requiring financial institutions and DNFBPs to obtain the information requested and to consider the information available based on the level of country risk, when determining in which countries such a third party can be based.

Financial institutions and DNFBPs should also have risk management systems to enable them to determine whether a beneficial owner of a customer is a foreign PEP or a family member or a close associate of one. If a beneficial owner falls into one of these categories, the financial institution or DNFBP must take additional measures to manage the risk. These measures include obtaining senior management approval before establishing or continuing with the customer relationship, establishing the beneficial owner's source of funds and source of wealth, and conducting enhanced ongoing monitoring of the customer relationship. They should also take reasonable measures to determine whether the beneficial owner of a customer is a domestic PEP and adopt the same risk management measures in higher-risk situations. Special measures are also required where a financial institution detects that a PEP is the beneficial owner entitled to the proceeds of a life insurance policy. See FATF (2013a) for detailed guidance on PEPs.

See Guiding Questions for Third-Party Reliance (Box 3.9).

Box 3.9. Guiding Questions: Third-Party Reliance

- Are obliged entities permitted to rely on third parties for conducting CDD, including the identification and verification of beneficial ownership information?
  - Which law/other enforceable means allows for third-party reliance?
  - What are the specific circumstances and conditions that permit financial institutions and DNFBPs to rely on third parties for conducting CDD, including the identification and verification of beneficial ownership information?
    - What measures are financial institutions and DNFBPs taking to identify the level of country risks of the third-party intermediaries on which they rely for CDD obligations, including identification of beneficial ownership information (that is, country risk assessments by the authorities)?
    - Do supervisory authorities check that these measures are adequate?
  - Does the law/other enforceable means specify the type of entities and professions that could be relied upon as third parties?
  - Are there any circumstances in which reliance on third parties is excluded altogether? What are these circumstances?
- Is implementation of reliance on third parties assessed as part of anti–money laundering and combating the financing of terrorism supervision?
  - Do checks specifically extend to beneficial ownership information?

Cooperation with Other Competent Authorities

Legal persons should be available to provide beneficial ownership information to different types of authorities in the context of other activities and policy agendas. These authorities should also have direct access to beneficial ownership information held by the public authority/body or via an alternative mechanism.

Numerous authorities have a legal need for obtaining information on ownership and control of legal persons for various reasons besides AML/CFT—for example, tax authorities are likely to always need some information on legal persons to determine tax liabilities; procurement authorities might require beneficial ownership information in the context of granting procurement contracts; and supervisors of the financial and nonfinancial sectors will have an interest in knowing who is the beneficial owner of legal persons that they supervise (for example, fitness and propriety issues related to banks). See Chapter 4 for broader applications of beneficial ownership information.

The FATF standards explicitly recognize the importance of having beneficial ownership information available in the course of public procurement. The standards require countries to ensure that public authorities at the national level and others as appropriate, have access to basic and beneficial ownership in the course of public procurement (see discussion in Chapter 4).

Legal persons should cooperate in a timely manner with all relevant government authorities in respect of providing information on their beneficial ownership and control during their day-to-day operations. Their duty to cooperate is complemented by the powers granted to competent authorities to obtain timely access to the basic and beneficial ownership information held by relevant parties and sanctioning powers.

These competent authorities should also be able to access beneficial ownership information held by the public authority/body or alternative mechanism. Countries should consider giving relevant competent authorities direct access to this information to streamline processes and reduce the need for beneficial ownership information on the same company being collected more than once by different competent authorities unnecessarily. This can help reduce bureaucratic red tape and also remove opportunities for corruption (when different agencies are collecting the same information, each having an opportunity to extract bribes from the company).

Changes during the Life Cycle of a Legal Person

Beneficial ownership information can change during the life cycle of a legal person. There should be clear rules in place as to when these updates should be provided, depending on how the beneficial ownership is being held.

Once basic and beneficial ownership information has been collected and verified, a system of ongoing monitoring needs to be in place to ensure that the information is kept current in line with FATF requirements. Accordingly, countries should ensure that there are clear requirements to keep information updated within explicit time frames and penalties for not doing so. In addition, historical beneficial ownership information should be maintained as a best practice to ensure a full audit trail.

Information should be updated as and when changes are being made to a legal person (for example, when there are changes in control or ownership structures):

- For legal persons themselves, this should be done promptly at the time of the change. This can be challenging for changes higher up the chain of ownership or in foreign jurisdictions because a beneficial owner at the end of the chain can be several stages removed from the legal person. In addition, legal persons might not necessarily become immediately aware of changes in their ownership—for example, the transfer of shares by way of a testamentary disposition or via intestacy might not be immediately apparent. This can be even more challenging with respect to changes in control of the legal persons. Notwithstanding, legal persons are required to know their beneficial owners and therefore should have systems in place for this information to be updated/shared by relevant shareholders.

- For gatekeepers involved in the creation of legal persons or providing other services related to the legal person, updating information will depend on the legal situation and whether they are required to be involved in any of the changes (for example, if the law requires notaries to validate a voting rights transfer). In such instances, they need to update their records at the time of initiating the changes and pass this information along to the relevant authorities. For registries and all other alternative mechanisms, there should (as a good practice) be strict time limits imposed by law (for example, within two weeks or one month) by which all relevant parties need to update beneficial ownership information (for example, the legal person, the gatekeepers, the beneficial owner themselves) and penalties that apply if this is not done within the time frame. This should include information on changes to ownership and control and for changes that come about by operation of law (for example, insolvency, inheritance, and so on). The information to be provided and who is responsible for providing these updates should be clear in each country.

- For other financial institutions and DNFBPs with legal persons as clients (aside from gatekeepers), the CDD provisions in the international standards require ongoing due diligence. This includes the need to update documents, data, or information collected as part of the CDD process. The reliability of the information obtained when there are changes in ownership or control of a legal person will depend partly on how well the financial institution or DNFBP is applying the requirements. But other factors might affect the reliability of the information, such as whether the financial institution or DNFBP has an active ongoing business relationship whereby they are in regular contact with the legal person. Relying on this as the only way of updating beneficial ownership information is not recommended, and countries that relied on financial institutions and DNFBPs to hold beneficial ownership information before the introduction of the registry/alternative mechanism requirement need to update their systems.

Changes to information should be submitted, updated, and stored automatically (if possible, via online systems) as a good practice, along with a regular requirement to verify information (for example, by requiring companies to verify and recertify information held in a company registry as part of their annual reporting cycle). Companies and/or gatekeepers that do not update the information in a timely manner should be subject to appropriate sanctions. Examples of such sanctions include companies being struck from registers (thus leaving them unable to officially carry on with business) and/or financial sanctions for failing to disclose changes. As a good practice, countries could consider requiring companies to have a named individual/officeholder in each legal person responsible for updating the information, with penalties for failing to do so (for small companies with one shareholder, that would be the same person). As part of the AML/CFT framework, sanctions also apply to other actors such as financial institutions and DNFBPs if they fail to maintain accurate beneficial ownership information as part of the CDD process.

See Guiding Questions for Adequacy, Accuracy, and Timeliness (Box 3.10).

Box 3.10. Guiding Questions: Adequacy, Accuracy, and Timeliness

These questions apply to legal persons, gatekeepers, public authorities, and other financial institutions and DNFBPs when collecting beneficial ownership information of dealing with legal persons.

- Is there a definition of what is meant by adequate, accurate, and up-to-date beneficial ownership information in the relevant legislation?
- What measures are in place to ensure that beneficial ownership information submitted is sufficient to identify the natural person or persons who are the beneficial owner or owners?
- What measures are in place to verify the identity and status of the beneficial ownership information? What documents, data, or information are used to ensure accuracy based on the specific risk level?
- Does legislation creating various types of legal persons explicitly require that basic and beneficial ownership information should be updated?
    - Does it include a time frame (how many days or weeks) for updating basic and/or beneficial ownership information when changes occur?
- Is there any guidance setting out an overview of steps to follow in updating relevant information, including which authorities should be informed of any changes to ensure that
    - Publicly available basic information is current?
    - Beneficial ownership information kept by the company is up to date?
    - Information in the beneficial ownership register, if any, is current?
- What measures are in place to verify and monitor implementation of the legal requirement to update basic and beneficial ownership information when changes occur?
- What sanctioning measures are taken for failure to obtain and hold adequate, accurate, and up-to-date beneficial ownership information?
    - Are sanctions effective, proportionate, and dissuasive?
    - How is it ensured that failures are addressed following a sanction?

Supervision and Monitoring

Effective supervision and monitoring mechanisms are key to ensuring that various stakeholders—including gatekeepers, financial institutions, and other DNFBPs—are carrying out their obligations with respect to beneficial ownership information. Supervisory resources and efforts should reflect the size of the sector, not the size of the country.

The various sources and methods of obtaining beneficial ownership information should be backed by robust monitoring and enforcement of the requirements.

This is a fundamental step in ensuring the availability and reliability of the information collected.

Monitoring of Companies

Countries often conduct a degree of general monitoring of companies and their activities, not necessarily related to AML/CFT. This might include checking that they still meet listing/capital adequacy requirements and extend to wider fraud-related checks. A register could have a reporting mechanism for activity that might be deemed suspicious (for example, if an individual has been appointed as a company officer without their knowledge or consent, if the registered office has been changed without the company's knowledge or consent, or if the company's name has been changed without permission). Although not directly related to the issue of beneficial ownership, this type of ongoing scrutiny of a legal person's activities can be a useful good practice in determining whether a legal person is being used for illicit purposes, and it can be a red flag to check that other information, such as beneficial ownership information, is still accurate. In general, though, many company registries face challenges with enforcing even these basic monitoring requirements.

Supervision or Monitoring of Gatekeepers

If countries require or allow companies to be formed by gatekeepers such as TCSPs, lawyers, notaries, and accountants, it is critical that these gatekeepers' activities be supervised appropriately and that enforcement action be taken where appropriate. AML/CFT assessments to date suggest that there are often technical deficiencies and effectiveness challenges when it comes to the application of AML/CFT measures by DNFBPs. For example, some sectors have yet to be brought into the AML/CFT system in some countries (such as lawyers and notaries) and even when there is formally a coverage, supervision of the sectors is often nascent (for example, regarding TCSPs). In some instances, this can be aggravated where countries permit self-regulatory bodies to monitor certain types of DNFBP (for example, notaries or lawyers can often be monitored by self-regulatory bodies). Where the self-regulatory body has a dual supervisory and representational function, there is a potential conflict of interest that can lead to a reluctance to sanction its own membership.

Countries with significant and well-developed corporate service provider sectors and countries that market themselves as hubs for international finance should ensure that they are dedicating appropriate resources for supervising these sectors. The resources and supervisory efforts should be in line with the size of the sector and the number of legal persons being incorporated in the country, regardless of the country's size. This can require a significant investment to enhance supervisory capacity and supervisors' efforts to conduct outreach and awareness raising in these key sectors. Supervisors should ensure that gatekeepers that are responsible for incorporating large volumes of legal persons are able to properly understand the ownership and/or control structures of these legal persons and are able to work with the beneficial ownership information of these legal persons regardless of whether they are complex or multijurisdictional structures. Under the FATF requirements, beneficial ownership information also needs to be held by a relevant public authority/body or a related alternative mechanism of that country, but this could also depend on the information that gatekeepers will be providing to the relevant authority/body or alternative mechanism.

Supervision of Financial Institutions and Other DNFBPs

Under the multipronged approach, countries should also rely on beneficial ownership information obtained by financial institutions and/or other types of DNFBPs than gatekeepers (for example, real estate agents). It is therefore important that supervision of these obliged entities also considers their ability to collect and hold adequate, accurate, and up-to-date beneficial ownership information. Results from AML/CFT assessments suggest that CDD requirements—especially in relation to beneficial ownership—are not always implemented effectively, because of confusion over definitions of beneficial ownership or financial institutions and DNFBPs' reluctance to look beyond legal ownership. In addition, supervisors do not always use an effective risk-based approach when overseeing sectors for which they are responsible. Again, it is important to have skilled and experienced staff both at financial institutions and DNFBPs and at the supervisor level. Beneficial ownership concepts can appear complex, and as a matter of practice, it is critical that staff involved at all levels of dealing with these issues are properly trained to deal with them. Supervisors also need appropriate powers to supervise and monitor, along with robust enforcement/sanctioning powers to act when a financial institution or DNFBP fails to meet the required standard.

Enforcement

Domestic Cooperation

> *Effective cooperation mechanisms among domestic authorities and/or centralized beneficial ownership information can help facilitate timely access to this information by all relevant competent authorities in the context of ongoing enforcement.*

Several different types of authorities will also require access to beneficial ownership information in the context of ongoing investigations into suspected illicit activities. These include—but are not limited to—law enforcement authorities, including FIUs, investigating and prosecuting money laundering and other crimes; intelligence bodies investigating national security issues; securities regulators investigating market manipulation, insider trading, or fraud; courts hearing cases of corporate self-dealing and other litigation cases; and public officials administering insolvency cases, public authorities involved in public procurement processes, among others.

Legal persons and all others holding beneficial ownership information should cooperate with all relevant government authorities in the context of these ongoing investigations and to the extent possible, avoiding tipping off any shareholders. Law enforcement and other relevant authorities should have all the necessary powers to obtain timely access to the basic and beneficial ownership information held by a legal person, the public authority/body or alternative mechanism, and financial institutions and DNFBPs.

The ability to share information among domestic authorities is important because certain agencies may possess or have better access to more accurate beneficial ownership information than is available to other domestic authorities for supervisory or law enforcement purposes. This can be extremely useful during the life cycle of a legal person because real-time information sharing is often necessary to investigate and prevent criminal activity (see Chapter 5).

Mechanisms, such as legal provisions or memorandums of understanding that allow domestic exchange of such information, facilitate the effective use of scarce resources and prevent duplicate efforts in obtaining the same information more than once from the same company. When possible, authorities should be given direct access to the relevant government and nongovernment databases because a cumbersome system for requesting access could lead to delays and undermine the usefulness of the information source. Competent authorities should also be encouraged to establish informal channels of communication and cooperation.

See Guiding Questions for Access to Information (Box 3.11).

Box 3.11. Guiding Questions: Access to Information

- Which authorities in the country have adequate powers to get access to basic and beneficial ownership information held by
    - One or more registers?
    - Financial institutions and designated nonfinancial businesses and professions?
    - Other competent authorities?
- Which law/other enforceable means set out the specific powers for individual authorities (for example, financial intelligence units, police, supervisors)? These might include general, non-anti-money-laundering-specific powers, but these might be perceived as less preferable.
- Which law/other enforceable means set out the general requirement that basic and/or beneficial ownership information should be made available to competent authorities either directly or upon request (for example, law on setting up a register of legal persons and/or a register of beneficial ownerships)?
    - Direct access
    - Indirect access
    - What are the formalities to be fulfilled, if any?
- Does the country have any cooperation/coordination mechanisms in place to facilitate access to beneficial ownership information (this might be part of an overarching coordination mechanism that is also used for other relevant aspects such as a risk assessment of legal persons), for instance, via focal points?
- Has the country consolidated ways in which to hold this information so that different authorities can have access to the same information?

International Cooperation

Domestic competent authorities should provide timely (in real time, if possible) access to beneficial ownership information for foreign competent authorities, including by using informal cooperation and channels for sharing intelligence information.

The ability to exchange information among different countries is critical because anonymity can be enhanced using corporate vehicles established in foreign countries. Criminals can use a chain of different companies incorporated in various jurisdictions to conceal their identities. It is therefore crucial that foreign competent authorities can access information on foreign legal persons created in or operating from other countries, especially in the context of ongoing investigations.

It is helpful for such investigations if countries determine that foreign legal persons (subject to the sufficiency test) are required to hold beneficial ownership information within the country. However, there will still be several instances in which competent authorities will need to reach out to other countries to obtain information on legal persons created/operating in those jurisdictions.

In this respect, the FATF standards require that foreign competent authorities can access basic information held by company registries and information held on shareholders. In addition, domestic competent authorities should use the powers available to them to obtain beneficial ownership information on behalf of foreign competent authorities.

Having public beneficial ownership registries in a country would be one of the quickest ways for foreign competent authorities to have access to information because they will not need to go through domestic counterparts to request this information. However, even then, cooperation between foreign competent authorities and domestic authorities would still be needed, including to follow up on any information in the beneficial ownership register if it appears that this information is not accurate.

As a good practice, assistance could be requested either through informal information and intelligence sharing or through formal mutual legal assistance in criminal matters. Informal information and intelligence sharing in this case refers to a broad category of information that law enforcement authorities, including FIUs, can obtain from their foreign counterparts, such as assistance in obtaining public documents and source searches, interviews with witnesses, and information in government databases. Seeking informal assistance before sending a formal request for mutual legal assistance could also ensure that the requests have a sufficient basis and are less likely to be delayed or rejected.

In cases where sources may not be accessible via informal channels, as a good practice, law enforcement authorities could seek formal mutual legal assistance in criminal matters or via regulator-to-regulator mechanisms, as established in formal agreements. Such formal assistance by foreign authorities can be provided for gathering evidence, obtaining testimony under oath, or executing searches and seizures.

As a starting point for effective international exchange of information, FATF recommends ensuring that foreign competent authorities—especially those that need to make frequent requests—have guidance on how they can access publicly available information (for example, a step-by-step guide). This would enable foreign competent authorities to check first whether the information is already accessible to them before making a formal request for information, such as through a mutual legal assistance request.

Countries should not impose unduly restrictive conditions on the exchange of information or assistance (for example, by claiming that such information is subject to tax or banking secrecy and other confidentiality rules). This could be included as a legal principle in relevant AML/CFT legislation, namely, to ensure that principles related to tax and banking secrecy do not apply as grounds for not sharing information on companies with foreign competent authorities in the context of AML/CFT and other criminal investigations related to legal persons. Where such considerations lie, additional guidance can be developed in terms of how this information can be shared with and used by the foreign competent authority. Note that beneficial ownership information is already public in several countries.

However, ensuring that this information is made available to foreign counterparts in a timely manner also depends largely on the way that beneficial ownership information is held in the country. Challenges can arise when the information is available only in a hard copy (rather than online), where an online system is difficult to access for technical reasons, or there is no central point of access for this information. To the extent possible, countries should consider providing foreign competent authorities with direct access to beneficial ownership information held by public authorities/bodies or through an alternative mechanism—especially if the information is held through a registry format. This information should be available to them without requiring any payment of fees or imposing any other restrictions on access to this information.

See Guiding Questions for International Cooperation (Box 3.12).

Box 3.12. Guiding Questions: International Cooperation

- What legal powers does each relevant competent authority (for example, registry, supervisor, financial intelligence unit, law enforcement) have to share information on
  - Basic and
  - Beneficial ownership?
- What are the formalities to be fulfilled for the information exchange (for example, formal written request), and do certain conditions apply (for example, description of a case that a foreign financial intelligence unit is analyzing with an indication of why basic and/or beneficial ownership information of a certain legal person is requested), if any?

(Continued)

Box 3.12. Continued

- Do any restrictions apply as to the use of basic and beneficial ownership information by the recipient counterpart (for example, after prior consent only)?
- Are there any other legal restrictions (for example, data privacy, banking secrecy, fiscal, tax laws)?
- Is information publicly available on the competent authority/agency responsible for responding to international requests for beneficial ownership information?

Access by Foreign Competent Authorities

- Which legal provisions permit access for foreign competent authorities?
  - Direct access (if information is publicly available through a public register)?
  - Indirect access based on a request?
    - What formalities need to be followed?
      - Request directed to the company
      - Request directed to a competent authority
      - Indication of the intended use of the information
- Do the legal provisions explicitly extend to information on shareholders?
- Do any additional conditions apply compared with the access to basic information set out above? For example, are costs incurred to the foreign competent authorities in the process?

Obtaining Beneficial Ownership Information on Behalf of Foreign Counterparts

- Which investigative powers apply?
- What is the source (that is, legal provision) for these powers?
- What conditions apply?

Quality of Assistance

- What measures is the country taking to monitor the quality of assistance they receive?
- How do you deal with the situation in which the request for assistance lacks necessary details to respond, and so on?
- Are there any uncooperative or problem jurisdictions?

Liquidation/Dissolution

Information on beneficial ownership should be maintained (preferably in a digital format and easily searchable repository) for five years or longer after the liquidation/dissolution of the legal person.

The end of the life cycle of a legal person is when the legal person is eventually dissolved/liquidated. This can extend far beyond the lifetime of a natural person.

Dissolution of a legal person does not mean that the requirement to maintain beneficial ownership information ends. The international standards require this information to remain available for at least five years after the date on which the legal person is dissolved or otherwise ceases to exist, or for financial institutions and DNFBPs, five years after the date on which the legal person ceases to be a customer of the professional intermediary or the financial institution. This follows more detailed record-keeping requirements for financial institutions as set out by FATF Recommendation 11.

The requirement extends to many of the organizations involved in obtaining and holding beneficial ownership information referred to here but also to administrators, liquidators, or other persons involved in the dissolution of the legal person. Countries should consider requiring this information to be kept for longer than five years, as a good practice, to preserve the trail for possible use by authorities who might need the information beyond the company's lifetime (for example, law enforcement authorities during investigations).

In addition, it is good practice that this information be digitized and the process be digitalized, maintained in a repository that is easily searchable and there is a data backup, with sufficient consideration for data security. Maintaining only hard copies of information is costly, and they can be easily lost or destroyed.

Liquidation can affect beneficial ownership, depending on the legal situation in a particular country. In the case of "normal" liquidation, the liquidator obtains control of the company's assets for the purpose of satisfying creditors' demands. At this stage, ownership and/or control by other means becomes less relevant.

Other types of potentially temporary measures that should not be confused with liquidation may have implications on beneficial ownership of a legal person. For example, some forms of insolvency protection do not fundamentally alter the beneficial ownership of a legal person. Countries should therefore take care to ensure that the end of a legal person's existence is not confused with some other form of potentially temporary measure.

See Guiding Questions for Maintaining Records (Box 3.13).

Box 3.13. Guiding Questions: Maintaining Records

- What are the record-keeping provisions that apply to
  - Public authorities/agencies involved in the liquidation/dissolution of various types of legal persons and the management of registries with basic and beneficial ownership information?
  - Any private sector bodies managing such registries?
  - Financial institutions and DNFBPs?
  - Competent authorities?
  - Legal persons themselves?
- Which law/other enforceable means set them out (for each)?
- Do relevant provisions require records to be kept for at least five years from
  - The date of dissolution?
  - The date a company ceases to be a customer?
- How are the records kept?
  - Is information easily searchable and can it be backed up easily?

Addressing Other Obstacles to Transparency

Bearer Shares and Bearer Share Warrants

> *Bearer shares and bearer share warrants, that is, physical instruments which confer ownership, are extremely difficult to trace. Countries are required to prohibit the issuance of new bearer shares and share warrants and to ensure traceability of any existing bearer shares and bearer share warrants through registration or immobilization.*

The use of bearer shares and bearer share warrants can obscure ownership of a legal person. In the case of bearer shares/share warrants, the person in physical possession of a share certificate/share warrant certificate is entitled to ownership and control and other interests in the legal persons (for example, payment of a dividend on presentation of a physical certificate). In addition, ownership can be transferred very easily by simply handing over the physical share/share warrant certificate (similar to transfer of cash). These certificates do not contain the names of the shareholders and are not registered, even though the ownership trail may sometimes be recorded on the share/share warrant certificate itself.

Bearer shares/share warrants may have had some limited advantages in the past, but their high level of anonymity results in significant enforcement challenges when abuse occurs. Possession of a bearer share does necessarily equate to beneficial ownership of a legal person, but establishing beneficial ownership in a legal person where bearer shares are used is extremely difficult because the shares can be held by anyone, anywhere, and without any trace.

Most countries have increasingly immobilized or dematerialized/registered bearer shares, with only very few countries still allowing such instruments.[11] The FATF recognized this, and in 2022, it required that countries prohibit the issuance of new bearer shares and bearer share warrants and take steps to register or immobilize any existing bearer shares and bearer share warrants—in line with the growing trend in this direction over the years. This is the best way to ensure that bearer shares and bearer share warrants or similar instruments without traceability can no longer be used to hide ownership and control of a legal person.

Therefore, countries should make amendments to relevant legislation to no longer allow the physical issuance and transfer of new bearer shares and bearer share warrants (if these were previously permitted under their legal framework) and ensure that measures are taken to register and dematerialize existing bearer shares. Countries should put a clear implementation plan in place to address

---

[11] Examples of country initiatives with respect to bearer shares are explored further in FATF (2019).

existing bearer shares in line with these legal requirements (for example, to establish a clear time frame by which the existing bearer shares need to be registered).

If countries choose to convert existing bearer shares into a registered form, they should clearly set out a reasonable time frame within which the relevant persons holding these shares must register them (for example, within two years). This process should align with the way other registered shares are held within a country.

Countries can also decide to immobilize bearer shares by requiring them to be held with a regulated financial institution or professional intermediary (for example, a licensed fiduciary) or national depository entity, which in turn should maintain a record of the ownership of the share and when any transfers are made. Where countries choose this option, supervisors have a key role in ensuring that the financial institution or professional intermediary is carrying out its obligations and holding this information on the record of ownership so that it is easily accessible and available to competent authorities in a timely manner. There should be clear requirements on when these records of ownership are to be updated upon transfer of ownership, and this should be done as soon as possible. Countries could implement legislation to ensure that a shareholder cannot use bearer shares unless the record of ownership is accurate and up to date.

In addition, while these shares are being converted or immobilized, countries should require all shareholders holding bearer instruments to notify the company, and for the company to record their identity before any rights associated with these shares can be exercised. This requirement to notify could also be extended to the national depository entity. Countries could also consider putting more stringent requirements in place such as the cancellation of shares without any compensation once the implementation deadline has passed.

Note that once a bearer share/share warrant has been registered or immobilized or there is a clear and traceable record of its ownership, it can no longer be considered a "bearer share or bearer share warrant," even if it continues to be called by that name in the law. The key point is that the concept of bearer shares and bearer share warrants needs to be removed from the law.

These requirements for newly issued or existing bearer shares do not apply with respect to companies listed on the stock exchange that will already be subject to disclosure requirements.

See Guiding Questions for Bearer Shares and Bearer Share Warrants (Box 3.14).

Box 3.14. Guiding Questions: Bearer Shares and Bearer Share Warrants

- Does a country's legal framework allow for bearer shares?
- Which of the mechanisms are used to mitigate the risks of bearer shares?

(Continued)

Box 3.14. Continued

Prohibiting the Issuance of New Bearer Shares and Share Warrants; and

- Does the country no longer allow for the issuance of new
  - Bearer shares?
  - Bearer share warrants?
- Which law/other enforceable means set this out?

One of the Following Options:

(a) Converting Bearer Shares and Share Warrants into Registered Form

- Does the country have a requirement in place that makes it an obligation to convert existing bearer shares/share warrants into registered shares/share warrants?
  - What is the legal basis?
  - What is the ultimate conversion date?
  - What is the process for bearer shareholders to follow to comply with disclosure duties—that is, shareholder identification and notification of beneficial ownerships?
  - What is the consequence if a shareholder by the deadline of conversion does not comply with the disclosure duties (for example, inability to exert shareholder rights, loss of dividend rights)?
  - Are there any sanctions that can be imposed on companies for breaches of the requirements to keep a shareholder register and obtain and hold beneficial ownership information?
    - Are sanctions effective, proportionate, and dissuasive?

(b) Immobilizing Bearer Shares and Share Warrants

- Does the country have a requirement in place that requires bearer shares/share warrants to be held with a regulated financial institution or designated nonfinancial business and profession (DNFBP)?
  - What is the legal basis?
  - Which financial institutions and/or DNFBPs are considered professional depositaries?
    - What conditions apply to them?
    - Is there a list of such professional depositaries?
- Are all professional depositaries subject to anti–money laundering and combating the financing of terrorism (AML/CFT) requirements, including beneficial ownership requirements?
- Is there adequate guidance for these professional depositories on the implementation of beneficial ownership requirements?
- Is there adequate guidance for these professional depositories on their role in the dematerialization process and ensuring transparency of legal persons and identification of beneficial ownership?
- Are implementation of beneficial ownership requirements assessed as part of AML/CFT supervision?
  - Are all categories of financial institutions and DNFBPs supervised for AML/CFT purposes?

- Do competent supervisors have adequate powers to sanction noncompliance with AML/CFT obligations, including with respect to bearer shares/bearer share warrants requirements?
  - Are sanctions effective, proportionate, and dissuasive?
- What measures are in place to ensure that deficiencies are addressed following sanctions?
- Are professional depositories under an obligation to provide beneficial ownership information to competent authorities in a timely manner?
  - Are there any exceptions (that is, professions that invoke legal privilege)?
  - Do certain conditions apply (for example, court orders, search warrants)?
- How do competent authorities obtain timely access to information on immobilized bearer shares or bearer share warrants held by financial institutions or professional intermediaries?

Other Requirements for Shareholders of Bearer Instruments

- Does the country have a requirement for bearer shareholders with a controlling interest to notify the company and for the company to record their identity?
  - What is the legal basis?
  - When is such notification to the company to be made? Is the recording in the company required before any rights associated with the bearer instrument can be exercised?
- Is there relevant guidance in the public domain? Is there any public awareness raising?
  - What is the consequence if shareholders do not comply with the requirement by the set deadline?
- What are the specific requirements for companies to comply with
  - Holding a register of shareholders?
  - Obtaining and holding beneficial ownership information and disclosing this information to the registry?
- Is there specific outreach to relevant companies on implementation?
- Which authority/agency monitors implementation of the requirements by the company?
  - What does the monitoring entail?
- Are there any sanctions that can be imposed on companies for breaches of the requirements to keep a shareholder register and obtain and hold beneficial ownership information?
  - Are sanctions effective, proportionate, and dissuasive?

Nominee Shareholders and Directors

> *Measures should be taken to mitigate the risks of misuse of nominees by requiring that information on the nominees and their nominators be available within the country and accessible to competent authorities.*

Nominee arrangements refer to situations in which an individual or several individuals (the nominator) issue instructions (directly or indirectly) to another individual (nominee) to act on their behalf either in the capacity of the director or a shareholder. Other terms used to refer to such nominees include shadow director, silent partner, or strawman, depending on their degree of formality. As the FATF and several others acknowledge, nominee arrangements—particularly informal ones—are a key vulnerability and are often identified in cases related to the misuse of legal persons. This issue has been covered widely, for example, in FATF and Egmont Group (2018) and most recently by the Stolen Asset Recovery Initiative (2022).

The FATF standards require countries to take steps to mitigate the risk of misuse of nominee shareholders and directors. These include outright prohibition of the use of nominee shareholders or nominee directors, or taking steps to ensure that information about the nominee shareholders or directors is more readily available in a country and accessible by the relevant competent authorities.

This can be done in one of two ways, either by:

- Requiring nominee shareholders and directors to disclose their nominee status (which should be public information) and the identity of their nominator to the company and to any relevant registry, and for this information to be obtained, held, or recorded by the public authority/body or alternative mechanism, or by

- Requiring nominee shareholders and directors to be licensed; for their nominee status and the identity of their nominator to be obtained, held, or recorded by the public authority/body or alternative mechanism, and for them to maintain information identifying their nominator and the natural person on whose behalf the nominee is ultimately acting; and to ensure that this information is available to the competent authorities upon request.

These requirements may necessitate amendments to relevant legal frameworks.

The public authority/body or alternative mechanism will need to hold information on the nominator based on either approach the authorities take. This information should be collected at the same time that beneficial ownership information is being required to be submitted to the public authority/body or alternative mechanism. Similar to the beneficial ownership, the information held on the nominator should help establish the nominator's identity (for example, passport and other identification documents) and proof of their nominee status (for example, formal documents outlining the nominee arrangement, any instructions issued by the nominator).

Natural or legal persons may already be licensed or registered as financial institutions or DNFBPs within that country and permitted to perform nominee activities. In such cases, the licensing requirement for nominees is not intended to create a new licensing/registration regime. The rationale for this is that financial institutions and DNFBPs would already be subject to the full range of obligations under the FATF recommendations, including to conduct CDD measures on their clients on behalf of whom they are acting. The standards make it clear that intermediaries acting in such capacity should comply with the requirements of FATF

Recommendations 22 and 28. The focus should be on supervisors to ensure that such licensed entities are holding adequate and accurate information on their nominator (who in many cases could also be the beneficial owner of the legal persons) and are able to share this information with competent authorities on request. Furthermore, it should be made clear to intermediaries that they cannot use legal or professional privilege to avoid disclosing this information.

See Guiding Questions for Nominee Shareholders and Directors (Box 3.15).

Box 3.15. Guiding Questions: Nominee Shareholders and Directors

- Does the country allow nominee shares and/or nominee directors?

One of the Following Options:

(a) Disclosure of Nominee Status and Identity of Nominator to the Company and to Any Relevant Registry

- Do provisions apply to both shareholders and directors?
- Which law/other enforceable means require this?
- What are the specific requirements for companies to comply with
    - Identifying any person who declares to be a nominee and hold shares or rights in the company on behalf of a beneficial owner?
    - Obtaining and verifying details about both the nominee and the nominator?
        - Obtain and hold beneficial ownership information?
        - Making a statement to the beneficial ownership registry, if any, containing the details of the nominee and nominator and identifying the nature of the nominee relationship?
- Is the nominee status of a shareholder or director included in public information?
- How can competent authorities, financial institutions, and designated nonfinancial businesses and professions access information on the identity of the nominator of the nominee shareholder or director?
- Which authority/agency monitors implementation of the requirements by the company?
    - What does the monitoring entail?
    - Are there any sanctions that can be imposed on companies for breaches of the requirements to keep a shareholder register and obtain and hold beneficial ownership information?
        - Are sanctions effective, proportionate, and dissuasive?

(b) Licensing Nominee Shareholders and Directors

- Which law/other enforceable means require that nominee shareholders and directors should be licensed?
- Which professions can be licensed to act as a nominated person?
    - Which is the licensing authority?
    - What is the process to be followed if a nominated person is removed or resigns?

(Continued)

Box 3.15. Continued

- Are these professions already subject to anti–money laundering and combating the financing of terrorism (AML/CFT) requirements (such as financial institutions and designated nonfinancial businesses and professions), including beneficial ownership requirements?
- Are these professions supervised for AML/CFT requirements?
  - Is the licensing authority the AML/CFT supervisor?
- Are they required to obtain the identity of their nominator and the natural person on whose behalf the nominee is ultimately acting?
- What obligations do these licensed entities have with respect to providing information to competent authorities on their nominee status, the identity of the nominator, and the identity of the natural person on whose behalf the nominee is ultimately acting?

(c) Prohibition on the Use of Nominee Shareholders or Nominee Directors

- Has the country prohibited the use of nominee shareholders and/or nominee directors, and if so, how has this been communicated?

REFERENCES

de Jong, Julia, Alexander Meyer, and Jeffrey Owens. 2017. "Using Blockchain for Transparent Beneficial Ownership Registers." International Tax Review (May 30). https://www.internationaltaxreview.com/article/2a68ya0zsexj3hc9hj0u8/using-blockchain-for-transparent-beneficial-ownership-registers

"Directive (EU) 2015/849 of the European Parliament and of the Council of 20 May 2015 on the Prevention of the Use of the Financial System for the Purposes of Money Laundering or Terrorist Financing, Amending Regulation (EU) No 648/2012 of the European Parliament and of the Council, and repealing Directive 2005/60/EC of the European Parliament and of the Council and Commission Directive 2006/70/EC." *Official Journal of the European Union* 2015 L141/73.

"Directive (EU) 2018/843 of the European Parliament and of the Council of 30 May 2018 amending Directive (EU) 2015/849 on the Prevention of the Use of the Financial System for the Purposes of Money Laundering or Terrorist Financing, and Amending Directives 2009/138/EC and 2013/36/EU." *Official Journal of the European Union* 2018 L156/43.

Financial Action Task Force (FATF). 2012. *International Standards on Combating Money Laundering and the Financing of Terrorism and Proliferation, Updated March 2022.* Paris: Financial Action Task Force. https://www.fatf-gafi.org/media/fatf/documents/recommendations/pdfs/FATF%20Recommendations%202012.pdf.

Financial Action Task Force (FATF). 2013a. "FATF Guidance: Politically Exposed Persons (Recommendations 12 and 22)." FATF, Paris. https://www.fatf-gafi.org/media/fatf/documents/recommendations/Guidance-PEP-Rec12-22.pdf

Financial Action Task Force (FATF). 2013b. "Money Laundering and Terrorist Financing Vulnerabilities of Legal Professionals." Financial Action Task Force, Paris. https://www.fatf-gafi.org/media/fatf/documents/reports/ML%20and%20TF%20vulnerabilities%20legal%20professionals.pdf.

Financial Action Task Force (FATF). 2019. "Best Practices on Beneficial Ownership for Legal Persons." Financial Action Task Force, Paris. https://www.fatf-gafi.org/media/fatf/documents/Best-Practices-Beneficial-Ownership-Legal-Persons.pdf.

Financial Action Task Force (FATF). 2021. "Procedures for the FATF Fourth Round of AML/CFT Mutual Evaluations." Financial Action Task Force, Paris. https://www.fatf-gafi.org/media/fatf/documents/methodology/FATF-4th-Round-Procedures.pdf.

Financial Action Task Force (FATF). n.d.-a. "Glossary of the FATF Recommendations." https://www.fatf-gafi.org/glossary/.

Financial Action Task Force (FATF). n.d.-b. "Revisions to Recommendation 24 and the Interpretive Note—Public Consultation." Financial Action Task Force, Paris. https://www.fatf-gafi.org/media/fatf/documents/recommendations/pdfs/Pdf-file_R24-Beneficial-Ownership-Public-Consultation.pdf.

Financial Action Task Force and Egmont Group of Financial Intelligence Units (FATF and Egmont Group). 2018. "Concealment of Beneficial Ownership." Financial Action Task Force and Egmont Group, Paris. https://www.fatf-gafi.org/media/fatf/documents/reports/FATF-Egmont-Concealment-beneficial-ownership.pdf.

Lord, Jack. 2021. "State-Owned Enterprises: A New Frontier." *Open Ownership* (blog), January 12, 2021. https://www.openownership.org/en/blog/state-owned-enterprises-a-new-frontier/.

Open Ownership. 2021a. "The Open Ownership Principles." Open Ownership, Alexandria, VA. https://www.openownership.org/uploads/oo-guidance-open-ownership-principles-2021-07.pdf.

Open Ownership. 2021b. "Using Beneficial Ownership Data for National Security." Open Ownership, Alexandria, VA. https://openownershiporgprod-1b54.kxcdn.com/media/documents/oo-briefing-using-bo-data-for-national-security-2021-12.pdf.

Open Ownership. n.d. "Beneficial Ownership Standard, v0.2." Open Ownership, Alexandria, VA. https://standard.openownership.org/en/0.2.0/.

Organisation for Economic Co-operation and Development (OECD). 2015. *Guidelines on Corporate Governance of State-Owned Enterprises, 2015 Edition.* Paris: OECD Publishing. https://read.oecd-ilibrary.org/governance/oecd-guidelines-on-corporate-governance-of-state-owned-enterprises-2015_9789264244160-en#page1.

Organisation for Economic Co-operation and Development (OECD). 2018. *State-Owned Enterprises and Corruption: What Are the Risks and What Can Be Done?* Paris: OECD Publishing. https://read.oecd-ilibrary.org/governance/state-owned-enterprises-and-corruption_9789264303058-en#page4.

Organisation for Economic Co-operation and Development (OECD). 2021. *Ownership and Governance of State-Owned Enterprises: A Compendium of National Practices 2021.* Paris: Organisation for Economic Co-operation and Development. https://www.oecd.org/corporate/Ownership-and-Governance-of-State-Owned-Enterprises-A-Compendium-of-National-Practices-2021.pdf.

Stolen Asset Recovery Initiative (StAR). 2022. "Signatures for Sale: How Nominee Services for Shell Companies Are Abused to Conceal Beneficial Owners." Stolen Asset Recovery Initiative, Washington. https://star.worldbank.org/publications/signatures-sale-how-nominee-services-shell-companies-are-abused-conceal-beneficial.

United Kingdom Department for Trade and Industry (DTI) and HM Treasury. 2022. "Regulatory Impact Analysis Disclosure of Beneficial Ownership of Unlisted Companies." Department for Trade and Industry and HM Treasury, London. http://webarchive.nationalarchives.gov.uk/+/http://www.hm-treasury.gov.uk/media/9/9/ownership_long.pdf.

Vaidyanathan, K. N., Akshay Mathur, and Purvaja Modak. 2018. *An International Financial Architecture for Stability and Development: A Global Framework for Tracing Beneficial Ownership.* Consejo Argentino para las Relaciones Internacionales, Buenos Aires. https://t20argentina.org/wp-content/uploads/2018/06/TF9.9.8-Final.pdf.

CHAPTER 4

Other Applications for Beneficial Ownership Information

Maintaining beneficial ownership information reaps benefits beyond tracking money laundering and terrorist financing. In particular, it can also support efforts to fight tax evasion, corruption and, more broadly, tackle illicit financial flows. Countries should adopt a coordinated approach to their understanding of beneficial ownership, given the relevance of beneficial ownership for several other compliance and transparency-related initiatives, and for the economy.

OVERVIEW

The availability of accurate and up-to-date beneficial ownership information is important for several other policy objectives and legal, regulatory, and operational frameworks in a country that benefit the economy. These include broader compliance and transparency initiatives, such as tax transparency, fit and proper (F&P) requirements, transparency for third-party lending and creditor rights, asset disclosure frameworks, procurement processes, extractive sectors, and for sanction regimes, among others. The Financial Action Task Force (FATF) standards cover some of these issues, and different global and sectoral standards and initiatives cover others. This chapter illustrates the multiple applications for beneficial ownership information.

Once a country develops a comprehensive and FATF-compliant definition of beneficial owner in the context of its legal framework for anti–money laundering and combating the financing of terrorism (AML/CFT), it is helpful to cross-reference this definition in other relevant laws and procedures related to these various initiatives. It is important to have one shared understanding and legal concept of beneficial ownership and standardization in the way that this information is collected. Thus, having a centralized mechanism to hold verified beneficial ownership information can be helpful and used to fulfill multiple objectives.

Targeted Financial Sanctions

> *Countries should ensure that designated persons in sanctions lists are not able to hide their funds or assets through legal structures.*

Access to beneficial ownership information contributes to preventing, detecting, and deterring evasion of targeted financial sanctions, including for terrorist financing and proliferation financing. To move funds or other assets (for example, weapons or vehicles) within and between jurisdictions, terrorist organizations have sometimes misused land, air, and sea trade and relied on complex legal structures to hide the underlying beneficial owner. FATF (2019) provides examples of such misuse. Persons and entities subject to sanctions use intermediaries or front companies to layer or obfuscate ownership/control information of companies or hide their true identity. In some instances, these front companies can also be used to move money on behalf of sanctioned entities, thereby acting as de facto banks for these entities. If the beneficial owners of legal companies are not accurately and timely identified, efforts to combat terrorist financing and proliferation financing could be circumvented.

Thus, effective implementation of targeted financial sanctions for terrorist financing and proliferation financing hinges on robust customer due diligence and ongoing monitoring by reporting entities, including the proper identification of their customers' beneficial owners. Having timely access to up-to-date and accurate beneficial ownership information when dealing with customers or transactions can help reporting entities identify if the beneficial owners of their clients are persons on sanctions lists. Competent authorities can also use beneficial ownership information in their investigations into violations and evasions of sanctions (Open Ownership 2021). Notably, countries that are unable to effectively implement targeted financial sanctions create a vulnerability for their financial sector that can negatively impact correspondent banking relationships.

The FATF standards are concerned with the implementation of targeted financial sanctions related to terrorist financing and proliferation financing, but the United Nations and other international bodies and many countries will also impose and apply sanctions for other reasons such as (regional) armed conflict, human rights abuses, and transnational anti-corruption measures. Access to beneficial ownership information is equally important in such cases.

Fit and Proper Requirements

Countries should ensure that criminals or their associates do not beneficially own or control financial institutions.

Financial institutions, designated nonfinancial businesses and professions, and virtual asset service providers are required to implement measures to ensure that their owners and controllers are F&P.[1] Supervisory authorities should also perform tests to assess the fitness and propriety of these owners and controllers. The focus of F&P checks is often on those directly involved in the activities/management of an entity (for example, the senior management or members of the board

---

[1] The FATF standards require that competent authorities or financial supervisors should take the necessary legal or regulatory measures to prevent criminals or their associates from holding (or being the beneficial owner of) a significant or controlling interest or holding a management function in a financial institution (FATF 2012). The same applies to other designated nonfinancial businesses and professions, for example, casinos (FATF 2012).

of directors), but requirements and checks to prohibit criminals and associates from being the beneficial owner are also important measures. For example, Basel Committee on Banking Supervision Principle 5 states that the licensing authority should identify and determine the suitability of the bank's major shareholders, including the ultimate beneficial owners and others that may exert significant influence (Basel Committee on Banking Supervsion 2012). It also assesses the transparency of the ownership structure, the sources of initial capital, and the ability of shareholders to provide additional financial support, where needed. Note that prudential supervisors will tend to focus on the ability and capacity of a person to own/control a financial institution, but for AML/CFT, the focus should be on ensuring the person's good standing (for example, that they are not criminals or cannot be subject to corruption or other types of influence).

The level of scrutiny on license applications (and ongoing checks) will vary depending on the significance of an entity (including the level of money laundering and terrorist financing risk); thus where F&P checks are carried out, they should extend to beneficial owners. For example, Basel Committee on Banking Supervision Principle 5 states that "the licensing authority should have the power to set criteria and reject applications for establishments that do not meet the criteria" (Basel Committee on Banking Supervision 2012). As such, the licensing authority has the scope to set the criteria, including imposing F&P requirements on beneficial owners.

Where applicable, F&P assessments of beneficial owners should be carried out at both the licensing stage and on an ongoing basis, including if there are any changes to the ownership/control structure. The review process should include collecting and assessing relevant information regarding F&P and AML/CFT considerations. More specifically, information should be sought on several criteria, including the beneficial owner's reputation and any potential risk of links to money laundering or terrorist financing. This information should contain details on criminal investigations or proceedings, relevant civil and administrative cases, open investigations, and the like. Once obtained, the information should be validated to ensure its veracity and completeness.

In circumstances where information casts doubt on the fitness and propriety of the beneficial owner (that may also give rise to the risk of links to money laundering or terrorist financing), the licensing/supervisory authority should have a policy in place to guide the decision-making process and to assist in determining whether to approve or reject the application. This process should give due regard to all relevant information, including open investigations and proceedings.

Transparency in Procurement

Identifying the beneficial owners of companies that are awarded important procurement contracts can help improve transparency in public procurement.

In general, procuring agencies and the general public benefit from knowing the beneficial owners of companies that are contracted to deliver public goods and services. Fairness and efficiency of public spending is better assured if companies compete on the strength of their bids and not because of extraneous factors, such as the personal relationship of the company's beneficial owner with the official responsible for approving procurement contracts. The procuring agencies' improved understanding of the natural person behind a company bidding for contracts helps them detect any conflict of interest, collusion, fraud, or even corruption in public procurement.

The FATF standards include as a requirement the need to ensure that public authorities have timely access to basic and beneficial ownership information on legal persons during the process of public procurement. To this end, bidding companies should be required to submit adequate, accurate, and up-to-date beneficial ownership information to the procurement authority, including any changes of beneficial ownership after the contract award. This should be a requirement for participating in public procurement contracts, leveraging the different approaches in the jurisdiction for reporting beneficial ownership information, such as a centralized registry. This does not impose any additional burden on the legal persons because they will already be expected to hold this information themselves and should also submit this information to banks when opening bank accounts.

Procurement agencies should consider undertaking reasonable due diligence efforts in checking the beneficial ownership information submitted by bidding companies and implement additional scrutiny and/or relevant sanctions if any observable red flags or suspicions of inaccuracies are detected (for example, inconsistent information, forged documents, or the beneficial owner is not a natural person) against the beneficial ownership information to which they were given access.

Beneficial ownership information of awarded companies should be published, in line with commitments made by many countries. Public access to this information also allows civil society and journalists to better monitor and scrutinize the awarding of procurement contracts and their implementation. The IMF has been encouraging countries to commit to publishing beneficial ownership information of companies awarded procurement contracts, including in the context of emergency COVID-19 lending (IMF 2021).

Tax Transparency

> *Countries should ensure that legal persons are not misused to evade taxes or abuse their tax responsibilities through domestic or international structures.*

Criminals can use legal structures (for example, shell companies) to obfuscate ownership structures to hide their wealth from the purview of tax authorities and evade taxes. Transparency of beneficial ownership information can help tax authorities identify the assets and wealth owned by a natural person and thus adequately determine the applicable tax liabilities, thereby helping jurisdictions preserve the integrity and the fairness of their tax systems and achieve their tax goals.

Ensuring tax compliance in the globalized world of finance and movement of people requires close international cooperation to prevent tax evaders from hiding their untaxed proceeds abroad. To this end, the Group of Twenty tasked the Global Forum on Transparency and Exchange of Information for Tax Purposes to ensure that its members and other relevant jurisdictions implement international tax transparency standards effectively and thus support domestic enforcement of tax liabilities. Thus, under its two tax transparency standards (the Exchange of Information on Request Standard and Automatic Exchange of Information Standard), the Global Forum requires jurisdictions to exchange a wide range of tax-relevant information—including beneficial ownership information (as defined under the FATF recommendations)—on foreign taxpayers with the jurisdictions of their tax residence (Global Forum and IDB 2021).

Under the Exchange of Information on Request Standard, tax authorities are required to provide to their foreign counterparts on request any information (including beneficial ownership information) that is foreseeably relevant for the administration or enforcement of their domestic tax laws or for carrying out the provisions of a relevant tax agreement. The standard requires that information be exchanged as relevant for tax purposes, which means that the scope of the beneficial ownership information exchanged may differ from that otherwise collected pursuant to the FATF standards (even if the definition is the same).

The Exchange of Information on Request Standard requires that up-to-date beneficial ownership information be available for all legal persons considered relevant from a tax perspective and for all bank accounts. Similarly, the standard requires that beneficial ownership information be collected on foreign entities with a sufficient tax nexus with the jurisdictions (for example, foreign companies that are tax resident in a jurisdiction by virtue of their place of effective management or administration in that jurisdiction).

The Automatic Exchange of Information Standard, which comprises the Common Reporting Standard,[2] provides for the automatic exchange of a predefined set of financial account information between tax authorities regarding the accounts of foreign tax residents. In situations that are considered higher risk for tax evasion, the information exchanged needs to include both the information on the account holder and its "controlling person(s)." The term "controlling person" has the same meaning as beneficial owner under the FATF standards, which is helpful, given that the Automatic Exchange of Information Standard leverages on the information that is required to be collected under the domestic AML/CFT framework. The situations in which information on the "controlling persons" needs to be exchanged are defined under the standard and include cases in which the entity account holder's business generates mostly passive income flows (for example, dividends, interest, or royalties). This is because such entities may not have a strong nexus with the jurisdiction where they operate, and there is a higher

---

[2] The Common Reporting Standard sets out the model due diligence and reporting rules for financial institutions to follow when collecting and reporting information to domestic tax authorities.

risk that they are misused to evade taxes. The United States also carries out automatic exchange of financial account information by implementing the Foreign Account Tax Compliance Act, which includes the same provisions related to "controlling persons."

Third-Party Lending and Creditors' Rights

Availability of beneficial ownership information matters for prudential supervision.

An appropriate understanding of the beneficial ownership of legal persons is also important for supervisory authorities from a prudential point of view. Banking supervisors are also required to monitor transactions between banks and their related parties and ensure that these are carried out on an arm's-length basis. This is a requirement under Basel Committee on Banking Supervision (2012), Principle 20. There are usually statutory limits on exposures to related persons and mandatory write-offs that must be monitored for compliance. Understanding the beneficial ownership of legal persons in commercial relationships with the bank assists supervisory authorities in identifying undisclosed related parties and associated transactions. Access to beneficial ownership information is also important to authorized securities service providers and their regulators to both ensure compliance with anti–money laundering obligations and guard against fraud and market abuse, such as insider trading (IOSCO 2004).

Beneficial ownership information is also important to both the public and private sectors in commercial transactions. A creditor institution will want to know the beneficial owners behind a corporate entity. Given the ease of incorporation, it would be possible for the beneficial owners of a defaulting company to incorporate a new entity and seek credit from the same creditor. If the information on the commonality of the beneficial owners were available to that institution, it might consider the credit decision in a different light. Similarly, credit bureaus, which specialize in assessing the creditworthiness of consumers, may wish to incorporate beneficial ownership information into their analysis and scoring processes.

Beneficial ownership information can also be a critical part of the due diligence exercise performed for issuing loan and demand guarantees. Banks can use available beneficial ownership information on the borrower/applicant (as their customer) to detect fraud or impropriety (see, for example, Wolfsberg Group, ICC, and BAFT [2019]). Parties involved in commercial transactions—especially lending, capital raising activities, and joint ventures—could also incorporate beneficial ownership information into their due diligence processes as a precursor to entering into a significant relationship with a corporate entity. Similar considerations arise for governmental entities in their contracting and procurement processes to ensure that risks of fraud, corruption, and other forms of reputational damage are identified and contained.

Asset Disclosure Frameworks

> *Countries should ensure that public officials do not hide any illicit wealth through assets that they beneficially own or control.*

Asset disclosure regimes are those requiring a certain group of public officials,[3] generally those in high-level and higher-risk positions, to periodically submit detailed information to a government authority on their incomes, assets, liabilities, and interests.[4] Typically, the mandated government authority should also verify this information, and it should be published to facilitate its use for accountability and enhanced social monitoring. Broadly, the objective of these regimes is to capture information and monitor the wealth of public officials across time to detect unusual or unexplained assets or income (unexplained wealth) and/or seek information to prevent private interests from influencing public decisions (conflict of interests).

The content of financial disclosure forms (the forms that public officials must complete to declare their personal information) can vary between countries and are constantly evolving, reflecting the shifting nature of corruption risks. Traditionally, financial disclosures required categories of information that would allow an individual to identify and value a public official's assets and interests. Over time, this has been extended to also consider assets and interests of close family members.

More recently, it has become evident that financial disclosures need to expand the notion of ownership to include assets and interests beneficially owned and controlled to ensure that public officials cannot hide behind a corporate veil—for example, if a public official owns a vacation home that is registered to a company of which they are the beneficial owner. Incorporating the concept of beneficial ownership can increase the usefulness of financial disclosures for anti-corruption purposes, facilitating corruption investigations, and the detection of potential conflicts of interest and also assist the financial sector when undertaking due diligence of politically exposed persons and support civil society involved in ensuring the integrity of public officials.[5]

---

[3] These can also be referred to as financial disclosure, income and asset declarations, wealth reporting, and interest declarations.

[4] Several international instruments—including the United Nations Convention against Corruption, the Inter-American Convention Against Corruption, the African Union Convention on Preventing and Combating Corruption, and the Arab Anti-Corruption Convention of 2010—include references and provisions on disclosure by public officials, making it a widely recognized tool. Additionally, regional and international documents have provided valuable guidance for implementation. Notably, Group of Twenty members endorsed common principles on financial disclosure in 2012 and on conflict of interest in 2018.

[5] For more on this topic, please see Rossi, Pop, and Berger (2017) and FATF (2021).

Extractive Industries

> *Knowing the beneficial ownership information of companies awarded extractive contracts can help promote transparency and accountability of high-risk sectors and improve natural resource governance.*

Extractive industries such as oil, gas, and mining are very lucrative both for extractive companies and the governments that award these contracts. The opportunities for corruption and bribe-taking in these sectors are significant, including bribery of public officials responsible for awarding these lucrative contracts, contracts awarded to companies owned or connected to politically exposed persons, and contracts awarded to companies that might overexploit or misuse the natural resources or engage in other questionable deals. Disclosure of beneficial ownership information can enhance the transparency of this sector, including by identifying the persons who ultimately benefit from it.

The Extractive Industries Transparency Initiative (EITI) is a public-private initiative that seeks to promote the open and accountable management of oil, gas, and mineral resources and greater transparency of these sectors, including by requiring the disclosure of information along the extractive industry value chain.[6] The EITI standard recommends that implementing countries maintain a publicly available register of the beneficial owners of the corporate entity or entities that apply for or hold a participating interest in an exploration or production oil, gas, or mining license or contract, including their identities, the level of ownership, and details about how ownership or control is exerted (EITI 2019). They are required to document the government's policy and multistakeholder group's discussion on disclosure of beneficial ownership and to request and publicly disclose beneficial ownership information of these companies (since January 2020). Additionally, a multistakeholder group should assess any existing mechanisms for ensuring the reliability of beneficial ownership information and agree on an approach for corporate entities to ensure the accuracy of the beneficial ownership information they provide.[7]

EITI suggests a broad definition of beneficial ownership, but it also introduces an element of subjectivity among countries, noting that multistakeholder groups should agree on an appropriate definition of beneficial owners for their countries—including by exploring international norms and relevant national laws—and should include ownership thresholds. This can introduce variance

---

[6] For more information, visit the Extractive Industries Transparency Initiative (EITI) website at https://eiti.org/.

[7] Recommendation 2.5 of EITI (2019). This includes information about the identity of the beneficial owner, including name, nationality, country of residence, and if any of the beneficial owners are politically exposed persons. Implementing countries should also consider disclosing the national identity number, date of birth, residential or service address, and means of contact of the beneficial owners.

among countries on how to determine beneficial owners. In cases of countries that need to implement both FATF and EITI requirements, countries should follow the FATF definition of beneficial ownership and approach to identifying and verifying this information.

Furthermore, if countries maintain central and public beneficial ownership registries, then this could also be sufficient to satisfy the requirements under the EITI standard, whereas implementing EITI requirements alone would not be sufficient to meet the FATF requirements. Although EITI focuses on high-risk extractive sectors, note that similar risks are prevalent in other sectors such as defense and military, real estate, and infrastructure, which also would benefit from enhanced transparency of beneficial ownership information. Countries can identify such high-risk sectors through their national risk assessments or targeted risk assessments of legal persons.

REFERENCES

African Union. 2003. "African Union Convention on Preventing and Combating Corruption." African Union, Maputo, Mozambique. https://au.int/sites/default/files/treaties/36382-treaty -0028_-_african_union_convention_on_preventing_and_combating_corruption_e.pdf.

Basel Committee on Banking Supervision. 2012. "Core Principles for Effective Banking Supervision." Bank for International Settlements, Basel, Switzerland. https://www.bis.org /publ/bcbs230.pdf.

Extractive Industries Transparency Initiative (EITI). 2019. *The EITI Standard 2019.* Oslo: EITI International Secretariat. https://eiti.org/sites/default/files/attachments/eiti_standard2019 _a4_en.pdf.

Extractive Industries Transparency Initiative (EITI). n.d. "Beneficial Ownership: Knowing Who Owns and Controls Extractive Companies." Accessed April 2022. https://eiti.org /beneficial-ownership.

Financial Action Task Force (FATF). 2012. *International Standards on Combating Money Laundering and the Financing of Terrorism and Proliferation.* Paris: Financial Action Task Force. https://www.fatf-gafi.org/media/fatf/documents/recommendations/pdfs/FATF%20 Recommendations%202012.pdf.

Financial Action Task Force (FATF). 2013. "Methodology for Assessing Technical Compliance with the FATF Recommendations and the Effectiveness of AML/CFT Systems." Financial Action Task Force, Paris. https://www.fatf-gafi.org/media/fatf/documents/methodology /FATF%20Methodology%2022%20Feb%202013.pdf.

Financial Action Task Force (FATF). 2019. "Terrorist Financing Risk Assessment Guidance." Financial Action Task Force, Paris. https://www.fatf-gafi.org/media/fatf/documents/reports /Terrorist-Financing-Risk-Assessment-Guidance.pdf.

Financial Action Task Force (FATF). 2021. "Politically Exposed Persons (Recommendations 12 and 22)." Financial Action Task Force, Paris. https://www.fatf-gafi.org/media/fatf/documents /recommendations/Guidance-PEP-Rec12-22.pdf.

G20 Anti-Corruption Working Group (ACWG). 2012. "High-Level Principles on Asset Disclosure by Public Officials." Group of Twenty Anti-Corruption Working Group, Los Cabos, Mexico. https://www.unodc.org/documents/corruption/G20-Anti-Corruption-Resources/Thematic -Areas/Public-Sector-Integrity-and-Transparency/G20_High_Level_Principles_on_Asset _Disclosure_by_Public_Officials_2012.pdf.

Global Forum on Transparency and Exchange of Information for Tax Purposes (Global Forum). 2016. *Exchange of Information on Request: Handbook for Peer Reviews 2016–2020.* 3rd ed. Paris: OECD. https://www.oecd.org/tax/transparency/global-forum-handbook-2016.pdf.

Global Forum on Transparency and Exchange of Information for Tax Purposes and Inter-American Development Bank (Global Forum and IDB). 2021. *Building Effective Beneficial Ownership Frameworks: A Joint Global Forum and IDB Toolkit.* Washington, DC, and Paris: Inter-American Development Bank and Organisation for Economic Co-operation and Development. https://www.oecd.org/tax/transparency/documents/effective-beneficial-ownership-frameworks-toolkit_en.pdf.

Group of Twenty (G20). 2018. "G20 High-Level Principles for Preventing and Managing 'Conflict of Interest' in the Public Sector." Group of Twenty, Buenos Aires. https://www.unodc.org/documents/corruption/G20-Anti-Corruption-Resources/Thematic-Areas/Public-Sector-Integrity-and-Transparency/G20_High-Level_Principles_for_Preventing_and_Managing_Conflict_of_Interest_in_the_Public_Sector_2018.pdf.

International Monetary Fund (IMF). 2021. "How the IMF Is Promoting Transparent and Accountable Use of COVID-19 Financial Assistance." International Monetary Fund, Washington, DC. https://www.imf.org/en/About/Factsheets/Sheets/2020/04/30/how-imf-covid19-financial-help-is-used.

International Organization of Securities Commissions (OICV-IOSCO). 2004. "Principles on Client Identification and Beneficial Ownership for the Securities Industry." International Organization of Securities Commissions, Madrid. https://www.iosco.org/library/pubdocs/pdf/IOSCOPD167.pdf.

League of Arab States. 2010. "Arab Anti-Corruption Convention." League of Arab States, Cairo. https://star.worldbank.org/sites/star/files/Arab-Convention-Against-Corruption.pdf.

Open Ownership. 2021. "Using Beneficial Ownership Data for National Security." Open Ownership, Alexandria, VA. https://openownershipprod-1b54.kxcdn.com/media/documents/oo-briefing-using-bo-data-for-national-security-2021-12.pdf.

Organisation for Economic Co-operation and Development (OECD). 2014. *Standard for Automatic Exchange of Financial Account Information in Tax Matters.* Paris: OECD Publishing. https://www.oecd-ilibrary.org/docserver/9789264216525-en.pdf?expires=1652388975&id=id&accname=guest&checksum=F88FB681E3C5E761DE89A10466DE92E2.

Organization of American States (OAS). 1996. "Inter-American Convention against Corruption." Organization of American States, Washington, DC. https://www.oas.org/en/sla/dil/docs/inter_american_treaties_B-58_against_Corruption.pdf.

Rossi, Ivana M., Laura Pop, and Tammar Berger. 2017. *Getting the Full Picture on Public Officials: A How-to Guide for Effective Financial Disclosure.* Washington, DC: World Bank. https://openknowledge.worldbank.org/handle/10986/25735.

United Nations Office on Drugs and Crime (UNODC). 2003. "United Nations Convention against Corruption." United Nations Office on Drugs and Crime, Vienna, Austria. https://www.unodc.org/documents/treaties/UNCAC/Publications/Convention/08-50026_E.pdf.

Wolfsberg Group, International Chamber of Commerce (ICC), and Bankers Association for Finance and Trade (BAFT). 2019. *The Wolfsberg Group, ICC, and BAFT Trade Finance Principles, 2019 Amendment.* https://www.wolfsberg-principles.com/sites/default/files/wb/Trade%20Finance%20Principles%202019.pdf.

CHAPTER 5

Policy Considerations and Regulatory Impact

Countries developing a thorough system for obtaining, verifying, and holding beneficial ownership information should involve all stakeholders whose policies and work may be affected. A whole-of-government approach and bringing in the private sector can prevent bureaucratic overload and facilitate the adoption of new, trusted mechanisms for determining beneficial ownership.

Countries must consider several policy issues when developing and implementing a comprehensive system for obtaining, verifying, and holding beneficial ownership information. This chapter sets out some of these key considerations. Before adopting any new mechanisms, countries should ensure that adequate consultation takes place with standard setters and technical assistance providers.

STAKEHOLDERS

An effective system for obtaining and holding accurate beneficial ownership information on legal persons is likely to involve a wide range of stakeholders, so it is important for countries to adopt a whole-of-government approach when setting up the regime, especially given the importance of such information for many different sectors and processes. For example, it is likely that interested stakeholders from the public sector could include the following:

- Ministries and public authorities responsible for anti–money laundering and combating the financing of terrorism, company creation, legal drafting, and budget (for example, Ministry of Justice, Ministry of Economic Affairs, Ministry of Finance);

- Government trade/commercial departments (which have an interest in ensuring that countries remain competitive, including being attractive places to set up and run businesses);

- Company registrars (which might already be the recipients of basic information and can be used in the process of holding beneficial ownership information);

- Law enforcement and intelligence agencies, including financial intelligence units (which will need access to the information);

- Supervisors (who might need access to the information and will be monitoring or supervising possible users and collectors of the information); and

- Tax/revenue authorities (which are likely to interact with legal persons at various stages) and relevant authorities related to other transparency initiatives.

Countries should also involve the private sector as appropriate, including the following:

- Trust and company service providers and notaries, if they are involved in setting up legal persons in a country;
- Financial institutions and designated nonfinancial businesses and professions that need to identify and hold beneficial ownership information as part of their customer due diligence obligations and that would benefit from using a beneficial ownership registry; and
- Nongovernmental organizations working on issues related to transparency—some of these organizations have been instrumental in helping to set up beneficial ownership registries in some countries.

Countries choosing to hold beneficial ownership information in a registry format will need to decide which public authority/body leads and is ultimately responsible for setting up and operating the mechanisms for obtaining, verifying, holding, and ensuring access to beneficial ownership information on legal persons. In some instances, this might involve setting up an entirely new agency (although adding this responsibility to a well-functioning company registry or other existing registries may also work). This will vary from country to country, but whatever authority or body takes the lead should have the stature and budget (including manpower) needed to deliver the beneficial ownership regime.

Complexity of Jurisdiction's Legal Sector

The size and sophistication of the type of legal persons that can be created and operate in a country varies with each country. Each country should assess the money laundering and terrorist financing risks associated with all types of legal person created and operating in the country and should use the results to assess issues such as the scale of legal persons' international operations, the types of activities they undertake, and the purposes for which the legal person is used in the country. For example, some financial and incorporation centers have many banks and trust and company service providers engaged in forming and administering companies mainly for nonresident clients. Issues related to international cooperation can be particularly relevant in these countries because other countries might depend on them to collect beneficial ownership information.

With information on the size, sophistication, and level of risk that the legal persons sector presents, countries must make policy decisions about the complexity of the regime required to ensure that beneficial ownership information is collected, held, and made available and that the system is appropriately supervised.

Legal/Regulatory Changes

Legislative changes will be required, depending on the extent of the changes made. Some of this can take time to implement, particularly if revisions are required to the commercial code and other key pieces of legislation. A public authority/body identified to obtain and hold beneficial ownership information may need additional legal responsibilities and powers to pursue these objectives, such as verification requirements and sanctioning powers.

Time Frame

Countries should also consider the time needed to implement changes to an existing system, such as how long it takes to enact any required legislation and whether regulations or issuing guidance could achieve the same result. For example, if the legal requirements are in place but not implemented effectively, guidance might encourage and ensure implementation.

Internal and external considerations will influence the time frame. Internal factors include the capacity and funding of the relevant organizations that might be involved in the beneficial ownership system (such as hiring and training staff and purchasing software or hardware). External factors can include pressure from the international community through poor mutual evaluation results or, for some countries, through requirements of action plans agreed to with the Financial Action Task Force.

Information Related to Existing Legal Persons

Countries must consider how to manage existing legal persons in addition to newly formed legal persons, especially when setting up new systems. One system should cover both newly formed legal persons and existing legal persons. Processes will need be in place to update information on existing legal persons (for example, by providing a time frame in which existing legal persons need to submit the information). Countries must also, in the development of their systems, consider how to manage the inclusion of information on foreign legal persons, if they choose to hold beneficial ownership of foreign legal persons operating in the country. Possible legal requirements for submission of this information, awareness raising, and monitoring how existing legal persons will be required to comply with these requirements are also important considerations.

Resources and Technical Considerations

Costs and technical capacity should be considered when deciding whether to develop a new beneficial ownership information system or make adaptations to an to an existing system. The cost of setting up a new system, such as a central database, will have to be assigned to a particular authority/body. Development of such a system will incur costs through hardware and software purchases, and the need to hire staff with relevant technical capacity. The system might eventually become self-funding, for example, through fees for registration and/or access to information. Making changes to an existing system may initially be less costly, but risks resulting in greater costs and potential inefficiencies as the system becomes operational if not fit for purpose. The cost of doing business for the reporting entities is equally important (see Box 5.1). The costs of a beneficial ownership system will vary greatly between countries, depending on the existing systems, the scope of coverage, and the type of registry or mechanism the country chooses to adopt.

Access to beneficial ownership information held in a registry format might be free or involve a charge. The access charge should not be so substantial that it discourages using the registry. Access by domestic and foreign law enforcement and FIs/DNFBPs undertaking CDD obligations should be free.

Technical considerations involved with setting up a registry, whatever format it takes, include ensuring that information can be entered easily into the database and that the information is searchable and in a machine-readable/open-data format. Strong cybersecurity measures to avoid cyberattacks or fraud are also crucial, given the information's sensitivity. Other considerations include how to provide access to other relevant authorities, particularly if different types of databases in a country need to be interlinked.

Consolidation of Requirements

Introducing measures to increase the transparency of beneficial ownership is sometimes perceived to have a negative impact on the business climate because of the increased compliance costs associated with implementing beneficial ownership requirements. Arguments against increased transparency include concerns that countries could lose business to other countries with lower transparency standards. However, this approach and these arguments disregard the longer-term benefits of integrity in business and government. More transparency can help improve the ease of doing business in a country. Countries that encounter lower standards in other countries or insufficient cooperation from other countries should consider raising these issue with the Financial Action Task Force or with the relevant Financial Action Task Force–style regional body to see how the other country can be assisted in raising its standards through training, technical assistance, or peer pressure.

Incorrect implementation choices can have a negative regulatory impact if countries simply add new requirements to an existing regulatory framework or if introducing beneficial ownership requirements leads to additional levels of bureaucracy and the need for new competent authorities. Such increased bureaucracy and red tape can also provide more opportunities for soliciting bribes, which can discourage legitimate business from operating in a jurisdiction.

Many of these possible negative impacts can be mitigated. The implementation of beneficial ownership requirements can be used as an opportunity to rationalize company creation and registration procedures, create new efficiencies, and reduce the administration involved in company registration, while introducing effective beneficial ownership requirements. Consolidating requirements can also have efficiency gains (see Box 5.1).

Box 5.1. Consolidation of Registration Requirements into a Single Registration or Entry Point

Existing rules and regulations may require new legal persons to register with several government agencies and make use of specific gatekeepers. It is common for new companies to have to use a company registrar, notary, or company service provider and submit similar or identical information to company registries, chambers of commerce, tax authorities, market regulatory authorities, or other supervisors at many levels of government (for example, municipal, state, and federal).

For greater efficiency, governments can consider designating one competent authority as a single point for receiving information relating to the legal person (the entity required to receive all the necessary information from the legal person, verify it, and share it with other government entities, as needed). Sharing information among government entities allows government entities to match the shared information with their own databases and spot inconsistencies at an earlier stage.

While rationalizing information streams, authorities need to consider the quality of the information needed to counter the abuse of legal persons and who needs to have access to it. Information that some competent authorities have historically requested from legal persons may no longer need to be submitted (for example, because the information may have become public, and the government can retrieve it easily). Authorities should consider this as part of the risk analysis of legal persons that the Financial Action Task Force standards require (see "Risk Assessments of Legal Persons" in Chapter 2).

Good practice for countries that face the risk of bribery of public officials (especially relating to paying government employees to help navigate bureaucratic requirements) might include introducing a single registration point for legal persons because this will reduce the opportunities for such bribes. It will also reduce the cost of doing business, increase legal certainty for businesses, and reduce possible criminal legal liabilities for legal persons that might currently feel forced to pay bribes to avoid delays or be refused business opportunities.

A single registration or entry point for company creation and registration can reduce the overall regulatory burden for legal persons and minimize the additional costs of having to submit beneficial owner information to authorities. By doing so, authorities can use the introduction of beneficial ownership requirements and the legal and institutional changes that this requires as an opportunity to increase the country's competitiveness (including for doing business) by reducing financial institutions' cost and time burden and providing them with a reliable information source for a large number of domestic legal persons.

Source: IMF staff.

REFERENCES

Extractive Industries Transparency Initiative (EITI). n.d. "Beneficial Ownership: Knowing Who Owns and Controls Extractive Companies." https://eiti.org/beneficial-ownership.

Financial Action Task Force (FATF). 2014. "Guidance on Transparency and Beneficial Ownership." Financial Action Task Force, Paris. https://www.fatf-gafi.org/media/fatf/documents/reports/Guidance-transparency-beneficial-ownership.pdf.

Financial Action Task Force (FATF). 2019. "Best Practices on Beneficial Ownership for Legal Persons." Financial Action Task Force, Paris. https://www.fatf-gafi.org/media/fatf/documents/Best-Practices-Beneficial-Ownership-Legal-Persons.pdf.

Financial Action Task Force (FATF). n.d.-a. "Glossary of the FATF Recommendations." https://www.fatf-gafi.org/glossary/.

Financial Action Task Force (FATF). n.d.-b. "Revisions to Recommendation 24 and the Interpretive Note—Public Consultation." Financial Action Task Force, Paris. https://www.fatf-gafi.org/media/fatf/documents/recommendations/pdfs/Pdf-file_R24-Beneficial-Ownership-Public-Consultation.pdf.

Global Forum on Transparency and Exchange of Information for Tax Purposes (Global Forum). 2016. *Exchange of Information on Request: Handbook for Peer Reviews 2016–2020*. 3rd ed. Paris: Organisation for Economic Co-operation and Development. https://www.oecd.org/tax/transparency/global-forum-handbook-2016.pdf.

Global Forum on Transparency and Exchange of Information for Tax Purposes and Inter-American Development Bank (Global Forum and IDB). 2019. *A Beneficial Ownership Implementation Toolkit*. Washington, DC, and Paris: Inter-American Development Bank and Organisation for Economic Co-operation and Development. https://publications.iadb.org/publications/english/document/A_Beneficial_Ownership_Implementation_Toolkit_en_en.pdf.

International Monetary Fund (IMF). 2000. "Offshore Financial Centers." IMF Policy Paper, Washington, DC. https://www.imf.org/external/np/mae/oshore/2000/eng/back.htm.

Organisation for Economic Co-operation and Development (OECD). 2014. *Standard for Automatic Exchange of Financial Account Information in Tax Matters*. Paris: OECD Publishing. https://www.oecd-ilibrary.org/docserver/9789264216525-en.pdf?expires=1652388975&id=id&accname=guest&checksum=F88FB681E3C5E761DE89A10466DE92E2.

Appendix 1. Basic and Beneficial Ownership Information Checklists

OBJECTIVE OF THE IMPLEMENTATION CHECKLISTS

These comprehensive checklists compile the questions included throughout this guide and are designed for countries to use when developing, checking, or updating their regimes for obtaining and maintaining information on legal persons. For detailed explanations to support the guiding questions, please see the discussion in the referenced chapter and section.

Chapter 2 (Mapping of Legal Persons)

Appendix Box 1.1. Guiding Questions: Mapping of Legal Persons

Mapping Exercise

- Has the country carried out a mapping exercise that covers *all* legal persons that can be set up in the country or have sufficient links with it?
- Does this exercise capture any relevant recent changes in legislation, processes for the creation of legal persons, processes to ensure that basic and beneficial ownership information is obtained and maintained?
- Does the mapping exercise also cover legal persons having sufficient links in the country but established or created outside the country (for example, domestic registration of foreign legal persons)?
- Have all types of existing governing legislation, enforceable means, and guidance (for example, at federal, state, and supranational levels) been identified and taken into consideration?
- Does the country keep a comprehensive overview of all relevant laws and enforceable means providing the legal framework for legal persons that can be created? Is this overview publicly available? Where?
- Does it give a clear indication (for example, through links) of where to find the various laws and enforceable means, relevant articles of these laws and enforceable means, and so on?
- Did competent authorities issue any guidance targeting effective implementation by individuals and professionals creating and managing legal persons to ensure that individual persons and professionals have an adequate understanding of what information should be delivered (by the person initiating the creation of the legal person) or obtained (by the professional involved in the creation and management of the legal person)?

Features of Legal Persons

- Do the various laws and enforceable means clearly set out
    - All types of legal person(s) that can be set up under each of these laws and enforceable means?
    - The basic features of all types of legal persons?
- Is this information publicly available, and can all relevant aspects (for example, type, form, and basic features) be easily identified? Where?
- Are there any other means that the country relies on to assist with the identification of all types, forms, and basic features of legal persons (for example, a summary document by the authorities)?

Processes for Creation

- What is the process to follow for the creation of each type of legal person? (List each type and how it can be set up.)
    - Can this information on process be easily accessed?
    - Is this information publicly available?
- Are requirements on basic and beneficial ownership information clearly set out?
- Is there any relevant guidance for the public (for example, on identification data and documents to be provided)?
    - Where can it be found?

Public Availability of Information

- How is the information setting out the previously mentioned mechanisms, processes, and requirements made available to the public?
    - Is there guidance to the public on how to get access to this information?
    - Is access direct through one or more central/decentralized government websites or other online platforms?
- Is access free of charge? If not, what are the costs associated with this access?

Chapter 2 (Risk Assessments of Legal Persons)

Appendix Box 1.2. Guiding Questions: Risk Assessment of Legal Persons

Types of Risk Assessment

- Has the country carried out a national risk assessment, and does it contain an in-depth assessment of legal persons?
- If not part of the national risk assessment, has the country carried out a legal person's specific or sectoral risk assessment?
- Which authorities/agencies and/or private sector stakeholders participated in the specific or sectoral risk assessment (as part of the national risk assessment or otherwise)?
  - What was the scope of the risk assessment?
    - Does the study extend to all types of legal persons that can be set up in the country? If not, which types of legal persons did the risk assessment cover and not cover?
    - Does the risk assessment consider foreign legal persons that have sufficient links to the country? If so, what type of foreign legal persons did it consider and why?
- How are those conclusions shared with and disseminated to the relevant agencies and authorities and to the private sector (for example, publication, guidance, awareness-raising events)?
- How often is the risk assessment updated?

Methodology

- Did the country use a dedicated methodology?
  - Does the methodology distinguish between money laundering and terrorist financing?
    - What were the sources of information: quantitative versus qualitative (for example, statistics on suspicious transaction reports regarding the misuse of legal persons, financial intelligence unit case studies on the matter, conclusions reached in the national risk assessment or supranational risk assessment)?
    - Are threats and vulnerabilities distinguished adequately?
    - Does the methodology define risk ratings and contain details on how to determine the risk rating?
- Does the risk assessment contain information about the nature and scale of each type of legal person that can be set up in the country, such as the following?
  - Legal framework for each individual type of legal person;
  - Involvement of gatekeepers in the creation of the type of legal entity;
  - Lawful purposes (commercial and noncommercial) for which the type of legal person can be used or is usually used;
  - Limitations to the use of the type of legal person (that is, certain types of lawful activities in which the legal person cannot engage);
  - How common the type of legal person is, including the overall number and relative importance;

- Information on the availability of basic information and how it can be accessed;
- Information on the availability of beneficial ownership information, including the sources (for example, central register) and how it can be accessed; and
- The basis for including certain types of foreign legal persons in the risk assessment (criteria used to determine sufficiency links)?
- Does the risk assessment describe in sufficient detail the various scenarios of misuse of individual types of legal persons for money laundering or terrorist financing purposes?

  - Does it distinguish between domestic and international threats? Does the study identify a set of risk indicators (for example, cross-border activities, the use of cash, predicate offenses) with reference to the national risk assessment and/or other relevant risk assessments?
  - Do these allow for an adequate reflection of risk variations between different types of legal persons?
  - Is there a specific focus on the risk associated with the intervention of gatekeepers?
  - Does it address the risks related to third-party introducers?
  - Does it address the risks associated with nominee shareholders and directors?
  - Does it address the risks associated with bearer shares and bearer share warrants?
  - Is there a specific focus on the risk associated with foreign ownership?
  - Are data sufficiently detailed to identify the largest source countries for foreign ownership?

- What are the mitigation measures in place? A nonexhaustive list of examples of mitigation measures includes (and consideration should be given to the adequacy of these measures and whether there are any deficiencies that should be addressed):

  - The legal framework, including filing of basic and beneficial ownership information;
  - Accessible registers with basic and beneficial ownership information by FIs/DNFBPs and/or general public;
  - Supervisory efforts to ensure that legal requirements are implemented adequately (for example, oversight measures to ensure that legal persons obtain and hold information on their beneficial owners through an up-to-date register to be kept, if any, and file changes in a timely manner);
  - Anti–money laundering and combating the financing of terrorism (AML/CFT) preventive measures for obliged entities, including adequate beneficial ownership requirements; and
  - AML/CFT supervisory measures to ensure effective implementation of AML/CFT preventive measures by obliged entities.

- Does the risk assessment arrive at a residual risk rating, taking mitigation measures into account?
- What are the risk assessment's conclusions regarding residual money laundering and terrorist financing risks?

Foreign Legal Persons

- Has the country conducted a risk assessment that considers foreign legal persons with a sufficient link to the country?
- What factors were used to identify foreign legal persons with a sufficient link?
- What factors are considered with respect to risks of foreign legal persons with a sufficient link to the country?

Chapter 3 (Legal Persons Holding Information on Their Beneficial Owners)

Appendix Box 1.3. Guiding Questions: Legal Persons

- Is there a legal requirement for legal persons to obtain and hold adequate, accurate, and up-to-date information on their beneficial ownership?
  - Does it extend to all legal persons that can be created/incorporated/registered in the country? If not, what are the reasons for the exemptions, and are these justifiable?
  - Are there legal provisions to ensure that this also applies to all legal persons that are currently in existence and operating in a country and not just new legal persons that are to be created/incorporated/registered in the country?
  - Is there guidance for legal persons on the implementation of the requirement?
    - Does it include a definition and background information on the concept of beneficial ownership?
    - Is this information also held by gatekeepers (for example, trust and company service providers)?
    - Do legal persons have unrestricted power to request this information from shareholders?
- Are legal persons required to keep beneficial ownership information up to date, reflecting any changes within a reasonable period (for example, within one month or sooner)?
- Do legal persons maintain records of previous changes to ownership structures?
- What sanctioning measures are taken for failure to obtain and hold beneficial ownership information?
  - Can the legal person be held liable for failure to implement the requirement?
    - Who in the legal person can be held liable for failure to implement the requirement? What about when ownership and management are completely nonresident?
  - Are sanctions effective, proportionate, and dissuasive?
  - How is it ensured that failures are addressed following a sanction?
- What are the mechanisms in place to ensure that competent authorities can get timely access to the beneficial ownership information kept by the legal person?
  - Is there any guidance for competent authorities on their access to beneficial ownership information kept by/on behalf of legal persons?
  - Are legal persons required to cooperate fully with competent authorities, including by making their beneficial ownership information available in a timely manner (for example, within 24 hours upon request)?
  - How quickly can the information be obtained (on average)?
  - Are there any legal requirements and related sanctions to prevent legal persons from tipping off beneficial owners if competent authorities request this information?
- What are the mechanisms in place to ensure that legal persons provide financial institutions and designated nonfinancial businesses and professions with adequate, accurate, and up-to-date beneficial ownership information?

Chapter 3 (Registry Approach)

Appendix Box 1.4. Guiding Questions: Registry Approach

Type of Register

- Is there a register with beneficial ownership information on legal persons?
  - Is it a stand-alone register, or is it set up as part of another register (for example, a beneficial ownership register as part of the country's central register of all legal persons, or a beneficial ownership register kept by private sector bodies involved in the creation of legal persons [professional bodies representing notaries, trust and company service providers])?
  - Does the register cover all legal persons or industry-specific legal persons (for example, extractive companies, companies engaged in procurement)?
  - What is the legal basis for the beneficial ownership register?
  - Which authority/agency is responsible for the management of the beneficial ownership register?
  - Does this authority/agency have sufficient powers and adequate resources to take on this responsibility?
    - Financial resources to ensure adequate maintenance of the information technology infrastructure?
    - Human resources to ensure that information in the register remains accurate and up to date?
    - Are these human resources adequately trained on the concept of beneficial ownership and transparency of legal persons, more generally?
    - Are there any government oversight measures to ensure effective implementation if the register is kept and managed by private sector bodies?

Required Data

- What type of data are included in the register (for example, details on the legal person, personal data, chain of ownership)?
  - Does it extend to foreign legal persons with a sufficient link in the country?
  - Is a distinction made for sensitive data?
- How are data entered in the register?
  - Online by representatives of the legal person or gatekeepers involved in the creation and management of the legal person?
  - Manually by staff of the authority/agency in charge of the register?
  - What type of supporting documents should be provided (for example, proof of incorporation, passport or other identity document or national identification number for each of the beneficial owners)?
    - Are there specific measures to verify the identity of the beneficial owner being provided to the register and to verify the information submitted?
    - Are there specific measures in place to ensure reliability of these supporting documents when ownership and management are entirely nonresident?
- Is the data entered into the register in an open data format (for example, the Beneficial Ownership Data Standard)?

Verification and Discrepancy Reporting

- What measures are in place to verify, monitor, and ensure that data in the register are/remain adequate, accurate, and up to date?
  - At the time of creation of the legal person and at a later stage when changes occur?

- How is verification carried out? What documents are required for verification?
- Is a risk-based approach applied to verification of information?
- Are there any specific measures in place to identify nominees and/or strawmen?
- Are nominee shareholders and directors required to disclose their nominee status and the identity of their nominator in the registry?
- How often and how quickly should beneficial ownership information in the register be updated when changes occur?
- Are legal persons/registered agents required by law to update beneficial ownership information in the register when changes occur? What is the time frame for providing updated information (for example, within 30 days of the change occurring)?
- Are competent authorities and/or other entities using the register required to report discrepancies between the beneficial ownership information in the register and the beneficial ownership information in their records to the authority/agency in charge of the central register?
  - Does any guidance exist to report discrepancies?
  - Are stakeholders trained to take on this important role?
  - What enforcement mechanisms or penalties are imposed on entities using the register for failing to report discrepancies?
- What is the process for reporting these discrepancies, including timing of the reporting?

Penalties

- What actions are taken when no or incorrect beneficial ownership information is filed and/or changes in beneficial ownership are not reported?
  - Actions when no beneficial ownership information has been filed?
  - Actions when changes in beneficial ownership have not been reported?
- What actions are taken when beneficial ownership information filed is false?
- What sanctioning measures are taken for failure to file (updates to) or submission of false beneficial ownership information?
  - How is it ensured that failures are addressed following a sanction?

Access to Information

- How will this information be accessed? Online? Is a hard copy of the register available?
- Who has access to the information?
- What information can be accessed?
  - Are there any limitations to access by competent authorities?
  - Are there any limitations to access by obliged entities?
  - Are there any limitations to access by public authorities in the course of public procurement?
  - Are there any limitations/special requirements related to access by the general public?
- Are there any requirements for accessing the data?
  - Are potential users of the data required to pay a fee to access the data?
  - Are potential users of the data required to register or provide any form of identification to access the data?
- Is there any guidance to obliged entities on their access to the beneficial ownership register and the use of the information?
- How quickly can the information be accessed?

Chapter 3 (Additional Supplementary Measures—Information Held by Financial Institutions and Designated Nonfinancial Businesses and Professions)

Appendix Box 1.5. Guiding Questions: Financial Institutions and DNFBPs

- Are there adequate measures in place requiring reporting entities to take reasonable measures to understand the ownership and control structure of a legal person and to identify beneficial owners and verify their identity?
  - What is the relevant legal basis?
  - Do the same measures apply to both financial institutions and designated nonfinancial businesses and professions (DNFBPs), or are there differences?
  - Are there certain categories of financial institutions and/or DNFBPs that are not subject to beneficial ownership requirements?
- Is there adequate guidance for financial institutions and DNFBPs on the implementation of beneficial ownership requirements?
  - Does the guidance include a definition of beneficial ownership consistent with the FATF requirements and include concepts of both ownership and control?
  - Does the guidance focus on ensuring that beneficial ownership information remains accurate and up to date?
  - Does the guidance contain details on understanding the ownership and control structure of a legal person?
    - Do any thresholds apply?
    - Does it differentiate between domestic and foreign ownership?
  - Do financial institutions and DNFBPs receive training to enhance their understanding of the concept of beneficial ownership and what is expected from them in terms of identification of beneficial ownership?
- Is implementation of beneficial ownership requirements assessed as part of anti–money laundering and combating the financing of terrorism (AML/CFT) supervision?
  - Are all categories of financial institutions and DNFBPs supervised for AML/CFT purposes?
  - Is the implementation of beneficial ownership requirements part of off-site monitoring or on-site or targeted supervision?
  - Regarding beneficial ownership information, are checks in place to verify that financial institutions and DNFBPs hold accurate and up-to-date information on beneficial ownerships?
- Do all competent authorities have adequate powers to sanction noncompliance with AML/CFT obligations, including beneficial ownership requirements?
  - Which supervisors do not have (adequate) sanctioning powers?
  - Are sanctions effective, proportionate, and dissuasive?
- What measures are in place to ensure that deficiencies are addressed following sanctions?
  - Do competent authorities have powers to obtain timely access to beneficial ownership information kept by financial institutions and DNFBPs?
  - Do these powers extend to all types of financial institutions and DNFBPs? Are there any exceptions (that is, professions that invoke legal privilege)?
  - Do certain conditions apply to such access (for example, court orders, search warrants)?
  - How quickly can the information be obtained from financial institutions and DNFBPs?

- What measures are in place to inform supervisors of deficiencies in
  - Making beneficial ownership information available to competent authorities?
  - The scope of beneficial ownership information maintained by obliged entities?
- Do financial institutions and DNFBPs have access to beneficial ownership information if this is held by a public authority/body, and are there requirements for discrepancy reporting?

Chapter 3 (Creation and Registration)

Appendix Box 1.6. Guiding Questions: Basic Information

Company Registry

- Is it required by law or enforceable means that the relevant authority should collect *at a minimum* the basic information at the time of creation and incorporation of the legal person?
  - Which law or laws at the federal, state, or provincial level?
  - What type of supporting documents are requested to verify basic information (for example, passport or national identity document, national identification number [issued by social security system, tax, or other relevant authorities])?

Information to Be Recorded by Company Registry

- Is there one central registry at the federal level, or are there various registries at the state and/or provincial level?
- What is the legal basis for the central/decentralized registry/registries?
  - Which authorities/agencies are responsible for managing the central/various registry/registries?
  - Do the authorities/agencies have adequate resources to take on this responsibility?
- How are data on basic information entered in the registry/registries?
  - What additional measures, if any, are put in place to ensure that recording is accurate?
- What type of documents should be provided to support data submission?
- Are there specific measures in place to ensure the reliability of these supporting documents when ownership and management are entirely nonresident?
- Does the register record all the requisite basic information, namely:
  - Company name;
  - Proof of incorporation (for example, date of certificate of incorporation);
  - Legal form and status (for example, limited liability, limited by guarantee);
  - Address of registered office;
  - Basic regulating powers (for example, Articles of Association);
  - List of directors, including directors who are both natural and legal persons; and
  - Unique identifier such as a tax identification number or equivalent (where this exists).

Publicly Available Information

- Is it required by law that basic information should be publicly available?
- How can the information be accessed?
  - Directly through one or more (central/decentralized) registries or online platforms by external service providers?
    - Is access free of charge? If not, what are the costs associated with this access?
    - Is access unlimited, or are there any restrictions on access?
- In what language or languages is the information available? Is there a possibility to add a name in any language/script?

Information Held by Companies

- Is there a requirement for companies to maintain information in law or other enforceable means?

- Is there guidance for companies on the implementation of this requirement?
- Is the information maintained within the country at a location notified to the company registry?
- Which authority/agency monitors the implementation of this requirement?
- Does the authority/agency have the necessary powers to impose sanctions in case of breaches of this requirement?

Register of Shareholders or Members

- Is the register kept within the country?
- Who holds the register?
  - The company at its registered office?
  - The company at another location notified to the registry?
  - A third person designated by the company at a location notified to the registry?
    - If a third person, what is the relationship with the company?
    - If a third person, is it an obliged entity subject to anti–money laundering and combating the financing of terrorism requirements?
    - Is there a record of the number of shares held by each shareholder? What are the categories of shares (for example, ordinary shares, redeemable shares, preference shares)? What is the nature of voting rights (for example, one vote per share, one vote per shareholder, golden shares [with higher voting rights])?
    - In cases of nominee shareholders and directors, is their nominee status and identity of their nominator included in the company register?

Chapter 3 (Day-to-Day Interactions by a Legal Person)

Appendix Box 1.7. Guiding Questions: Third-Party Reliance

- Are obliged entities permitted to rely on third parties for conducting CDD, including the identification and verification of beneficial ownership information?
  - Which law/other enforceable means allows for third-party reliance?
  - What are the specific circumstances and conditions that permit financial institutions and DNFBPs to rely on third parties for conducting CDD, including the identification and verification of beneficial ownership information?
    - What measures are financial institutions and DNFBPs taking to identify the level of country risks of the third-party intermediaries on which they rely for CDD obligations, including identification of beneficial ownership information (that is, country risk assessments by the authorities)?
      - Do supervisory authorities check that these measures are adequate?
  - Does the law/other enforceable means specify the type of entities and professions that could be relied upon as third parties?
  - Are there any circumstances in which reliance on third parties is excluded altogether? What are these circumstances?
- Is implementation of reliance on third parties assessed as part of AML/CFT supervision?
  - Do checks specifically extend to beneficial ownership information?

Chapter 3 (Changes during the Life Cycle of a Legal Person)

Appendix Box 1.8. Guiding Questions: Adequacy, Accuracy, and Timeliness

These questions apply to legal persons, gatekeepers, public authorities, and other financial institutions and DNFBPs when collecting beneficial ownership information of dealing with legal persons.

- Is there a definition of what is meant by adequate, accurate, and up-to-date beneficial ownership information in the relevant legislation?
- What measures are in place to ensure that beneficial ownership information submitted is sufficient to identify the natural person or persons who are the beneficial owner or owners?
- What measures are in place to verify the identity and status of the beneficial ownership information? What documents, data, or information are used to ensure accuracy based on the specific risk level?
- Does legislation creating various types of legal persons explicitly require that basic and beneficial ownership information should be updated?
  - Does it include a time frame (how many days or weeks) for updating basic and/or beneficial ownership information when changes occur?
- Is there any guidance setting out an overview of steps to follow in updating relevant information, including which authorities should be informed of any changes to ensure that
  - Publicly available basic information is current?
  - Beneficial ownership information kept by the company is up to date?
  - Information in the beneficial ownership register, if any, is current?
- What measures are in place to verify and monitor implementation of the legal requirement to update basic and beneficial ownership information when changes occur?
- What sanctioning measures are taken for failure to obtain and hold adequate, accurate, and up-to-date beneficial ownership information?
  - Are sanctions effective, proportionate, and dissuasive?
  - How is it ensured that failures are addressed following a sanction?

Chapter 3 (Enforcement)

Appendix Box 1.9. Guiding Questions: Access to Information

- Which authorities in the country have adequate powers to get access to basic and beneficial ownership information held by
  - One or more registers?
  - Financial institutions and designated nonfinancial businesses and professions?
  - Other competent authorities?
- Which law/other enforceable means set out the specific powers for individual authorities (for example, financial intelligence units, police, supervisors)? These might include general, non-anti-money-laundering-specific powers, but these might be perceived as less preferable.
- Which law/other enforceable means set out the general requirement that basic and/or beneficial ownership information should be made available to competent authorities either directly or upon request (for example, law on setting up a register of legal persons and/or a register of beneficial ownerships)?
  - Direct access
  - Indirect access
  - What are the formalities to be fulfilled, if any?
- Does the country have any cooperation/coordination mechanisms in place to facilitate access to beneficial ownership information (this might be part of an overarching coordination mechanism that is also used for other relevant aspects such as a risk assessment of legal persons), for instance, via focal points?
- Has the country consolidated ways in which to hold this information so that different authorities can have access to the same information?

Appendix Box 1.10. Guiding Questions: International Cooperation

- What legal powers does each relevant competent authority (for example, registry, supervisor, financial intelligence unit, law enforcement) have to share information on
  - Basic and
  - Beneficial ownership?
- What are the formalities to be fulfilled for the information exchange (for example, formal written request), and do certain conditions apply (for example, description of a case that a foreign financial intelligence unit is analyzing with an indication of why basic and/or beneficial ownership information of a certain legal person is requested), if any?
- Do any restrictions apply as to the use of basic and beneficial ownership information by the recipient counterpart (for example, after prior consent only)?
- Are there any other legal restrictions (for example, data privacy, banking secrecy, fiscal, tax laws)?
- Is information publicly available on the competent authority/agency responsible for responding to international requests for beneficial ownership information?

Access by Foreign Competent Authorities

- Which legal provisions permit access for foreign competent authorities?
  - Direct access (if information is publicly available through a public register)?
  - Indirect access based on a request?
    - What formalities need to be followed?
      - Request directed to the company
      - Request directed to a competent authority
      - Indication of the intended use of the information
- Do the legal provisions explicitly extend to information on shareholders?
- Do any additional conditions apply compared with the access to basic information set out above? For example, are costs incurred to the foreign competent authorities in the process?

Obtaining Beneficial Ownership Information on Behalf of Foreign Counterparts

- Which investigative powers apply?
- What is the source (that is, legal provision) for these powers?
- What conditions apply?

Quality of Assistance

- What measures is the country taking to monitor the quality of assistance they receive?
- How do you deal with the situation in which the request for assistance lacks necessary details to respond, and so on?
- Are there any uncooperative or problem jurisdictions?

Chapter 3 (Liquidation/Dissolution)

Appendix Box 1.11. Guiding Questions: Maintaining Records

- What are the record-keeping provisions that apply to
  - Public authorities/agencies involved in the liquidation/dissolution of various types of legal persons and the management of registries with basic and beneficial ownership information?
  - Any private sector bodies managing such registries?
  - Financial institutions and DNFBPs?
  - Competent authorities?
  - Legal persons themselves?
- Which law/other enforceable means set them out (for each)?
- Do relevant provisions require records to be kept for at least five years from
  - The date of dissolution?
  - The date a company ceases to be a customer?
- How are the records kept?
  - Is information easily searchable and can it be backed up easily?

Chapter 3 (Bearer Shares/Share Warrants)

Appendix Box 1.12. Guiding Questions: Bearer Shares and Bearer Share Warrants

- Does a country's legal framework allow for bearer shares?
- Which of the mechanisms are used to mitigate the risks of bearer shares?

Prohibiting the Issuance of New Bearer Shares and Share Warrants; and

- Does the country no longer allow for the issuance of new
  - Bearer shares?
  - Bearer share warrants?
- Which law/other enforceable means set this out?

One of the Following Options:

(a) Converting Bearer Shares and Share Warrants into Registered Form

- Does the country have a requirement in place that makes it an obligation to convert existing bearer shares/share warrants into registered shares/share warrants?
  - What is the legal basis?
  - What is the ultimate conversion date?
  - What is the process for bearer shareholders to follow to comply with disclosure duties—that is, shareholder identification and notification of beneficial ownerships?
  - What is the consequence if a shareholder by the deadline of conversion does not comply with the disclosure duties (for example, inability to exert shareholder rights, loss of dividend rights)?
  - Are there any sanctions that can be imposed on companies for breaches of the requirements to keep a shareholder register and obtain and hold beneficial ownership information?
    - Are sanctions effective, proportionate, and dissuasive?

(b) Immobilizing Bearer Shares and Share Warrants

- Does the country have a requirement in place that requires bearer shares/share warrants to be held with a regulated financial institution or designated nonfinancial business and profession (DNFBP)?
  - What is the legal basis?
  - Which financial institutions and/or DNFBPs are considered professional depositaries?
    - What conditions apply to them?
    - Is there a list of such professional depositaries?
- Are all professional depositaries subject to anti–money laundering and combating the financing of terrorism (AML/CFT) requirements, including beneficial ownership requirements?
- Is there adequate guidance for these professional depositories on the implementation of beneficial ownership requirements?

- Is there adequate guidance for these professional depositories on their role in the dematerialization process and ensuring transparency of legal persons and identification of beneficial ownership?
- Are implementation of beneficial ownership requirements assessed as part of AML/CFT supervision?
    - Are all categories of financial institutions and DNFBPs supervised for AML/CFT purposes?
- Do competent supervisors have adequate powers to sanction noncompliance with AML/CFT obligations, including with respect to bearer shares/bearer share warrants requirements?
    - Are sanctions effective, proportionate, and dissuasive?
- What measures are in place to ensure that deficiencies are addressed following sanctions?
- Are professional depositories under an obligation to provide beneficial ownership information to competent authorities in a timely manner?
    - Are there any exceptions (that is, professions that invoke legal privilege)?
    - Do certain conditions apply (for example, court orders, search warrants)?
- How do competent authorities obtain timely access to information on immobilized bearer shares or bearer share warrants held by financial institutions or professional intermediaries?

Other Requirements for Shareholders of Bearer Instruments

- Does the country have a requirement for bearer shareholders with a controlling interest to notify the company and for the company to record their identity?
    - What is the legal basis?
    - When is such notification to the company to be made? Is the recording in the company required before any rights associated with the bearer instrument can be exercised?
- Is there relevant guidance in the public domain? Is there any public awareness raising?
    - What is the consequence if shareholders do not comply with the requirement by the set deadline?
- What are the specific requirements for companies to comply with
    - Holding a register of shareholders?
    - Obtaining and holding beneficial ownership information and disclosing this information to the registry?
- Is there specific outreach to relevant companies in view of implementation?
- Which authority/agency monitors implementation of the requirements by the company?
    - What does the monitoring entail?
- Are there any sanctions that can be imposed on companies for breaches of the requirements to keep a shareholder register and obtain and hold beneficial ownership information?
    - Are sanctions effective, proportionate, and dissuasive?

Chapter 3 (Nominee Shareholders and Directors)

Appendix Box 1.13. Guiding Questions: Nominee Shareholders and Directors

- Does the country allow nominee shares and/or nominee directors?

One of the Following Options

(a) Disclosure of Nominee Status and Identity of Nominator to the Company and to Any Relevant Registry

- Do provisions apply to both shareholders and directors?
- Which law/other enforceable means require this?
- What are the specific requirements for companies to comply with
  - Identifying any person who declares to be a nominee and hold shares or rights in the company on behalf of a beneficial owner?
  - Obtaining and verifying details about both the nominee and the nominator?
    - Obtain and hold beneficial ownership information?
    - Making a statement to the beneficial ownership registry, if any, containing the details of the nominee and nominator and identifying the nature of the nominee relationship?
- Is the nominee status of a shareholder or director included in public information?
- How can competent authorities, financial institutions, and designated nonfinancial businesses and professions access information on the identity of the nominator of the nominee shareholder or director?
- Which authority/agency monitors implementation of the requirements by the company?
  - What does the monitoring entail?
  - Are there any sanctions that can be imposed on companies for breaches of the requirements to keep a shareholder register and obtain and hold beneficial ownership information?
    - Are sanctions effective, proportionate, and dissuasive?

(b) Licensing Nominee Shareholders and Directors

- Which law/other enforceable means require that nominee shareholders and directors should be licensed?
- Which professions can be licensed to act as a nominated person?
  - Which is the licensing authority?
  - What is the process to be followed if a nominated person is removed or resigns?
  - Are these professions already subject to anti–money laundering and combating the financing of terrorism (AML/CFT) requirements (such as financial institutions and designated nonfinancial businesses and professions), including beneficial ownership requirements?
  - Are these professions supervised for AML/CFT requirements?
    - Is the licensing authority the AML/CFT supervisor?
  - Are they required to obtain the identity of their nominator and the natural person on whose behalf the nominee is ultimately acting?
  - What obligations do these licensed entities have with respect to providing information to competent authorities on their nominee status, the identity of the nominator, and the identity of the natural person on whose behalf the nominee is ultimately acting?

(c) Prohibition on the Use of Nominee Shareholders or Nominee Directors

- Has the country prohibited the use of nominee shareholders and/or nominee directors, and if so, how has this been communicated?

Appendix 2. FATF Standards, Recommendation 24, Transparency and Beneficial Ownership of Legal Persons

RECOMMENDATION 24. TRANSPARENCY AND BENEFICIAL OWNERSHIP OF LEGAL PERSONS

Countries should assess the risks of misuse of legal persons for money laundering or terrorist financing, and take measures to prevent their misuse. Countries should ensure that there is adequate, accurate and up-to-date information on the beneficial ownership and control of legal persons that can be obtained or accessed rapidly and efficiently by competent authorities, through either a register of beneficial ownership or an alternative mechanism. Countries should not permit legal persons to issue new bearer shares or bearer share warrants, and take measures to prevent the misuse of existing bearer shares and bearer share warrants. Countries should take effective measures to ensure that nominee shareholders and directors are not misused for money laundering or terrorist financing. Countries should consider facilitating access to beneficial ownership and control information by financial institutions and DNFBPs undertaking the requirements set out in Recommendations 10 and 22.

INTERPRETIVE NOTE TO RECOMMENDATION 24 (TRANSPARENCY AND BENEFICIAL OWNERSHIP OF LEGAL PERSONS)

1. Competent authorities should be able to obtain, or have access in a timely fashion to, adequate, accurate and up-to-date information on the beneficial ownership and control of companies and other legal persons (beneficial ownership information[1]) that are created[2] in the country, as well as those that

---

[1] Beneficial ownership information for legal persons is the information referred to in the interpretive note to Recommendation 10, paragraph 5(b)(i). Controlling shareholders as referred to in, paragraph 5(b)(i) of the interpretive note to Recommendation 10 may be based on a threshold, e.g. any persons owning more than a certain percentage of the company (determined based on the jurisdiction's assessment of risk, with a maximum of 25%).

[2] References to creating a legal person, include incorporation of companies or any other mechanism that is used.

present ML/TF risks and have sufficient links[3] with their country (if they are not created in the country). Countries may choose the mechanisms they rely on to achieve this objective, although they should also comply with the minimum requirements set out below. Countries should utilise a combination of mechanisms to achieve the objective.

2. As part of the process described in paragraph 1 of ensuring that there is adequate transparency regarding legal persons, countries should have mechanisms that:

   a) identify and describe the different types, forms and basic features of legal persons in the country;

   b) identify and describe the processes for: (i) the creation of those legal persons; and (ii) the obtaining and recording of basic and beneficial ownership information;

   c) make the above information publicly available;

   d) assess the money laundering and terrorist financing risks associated with different types of legal persons created in the country, and take appropriate steps to manage and mitigate the risks that they identify; and

   e) assess the money laundering and terrorist financing risks to which their country is exposed, associated with different types of foreign-created legal persons, and take appropriate steps to manage and mitigate the risks that they identify.[4]

A. Basic Information

3. In order to determine who the beneficial owners of a company[5] are, competent authorities will require certain basic information about the company, which, at a minimum, would include information about the legal ownership and control structure of the company. This would include information about the status and powers of the company, its shareholders and its directors.

4. All companies created in a country should be registered in a company registry.[6] Whichever combination of mechanisms is used to obtain and record

---

[3] Countries may determine what is considered a sufficient link on the basis of risk. Examples of sufficiency tests may include, but are not limited to, when a company has permanent establishment/branch/agency, has significant business activity or has significant and ongoing business relations with financial institutions or DNFBPs, subject to AML/CFT regulation, has significant real estate/other local investment, employs staff, or is a tax resident, in the country.

[4] This could be done through national and/or supranational measures. These could include requiring beneficial ownership information on some types of foreign-created legal persons to be held as set out under paragraph 7.

[5] Recommendation 24 applies to all forms of legal persons. The requirements are described primarily with reference to companies, but similar requirements should be applied to other types of legal person, taking into account their different forms and structures - as set out in Section E.

[6] "Company registry" refers to a register in the country of companies incorporated or licensed in that country and normally maintained by or for the incorporating authority. It does not refer to information held by or for the company itself.

beneficial ownership information (see section B), there is a set of basic information on a company that needs to be obtained and recorded by the company[7] as a necessary prerequisite. The minimum basic information to be obtained and recorded by a company should be:

a) company name, proof of incorporation, legal form and status, the address of the registered office, basic regulating powers (e.g. memorandum & articles of association), a list of directors, and unique identifier such as a tax identification number or equivalent (where this exists);[8] and

b) a register of its shareholders or members, containing the names of the shareholders and members and number of shares held by each shareholder[9] and categories of shares (including the nature of the associated voting rights).

5. The company registry[10] should record all the basic information set out in paragraph 4(a) above.

6. The company should maintain the basic information set out in paragraph 4(b) within the country, either at its registered office or at another location notified to the company registry. However, if the company or company registry holds beneficial ownership information within the country, then the register of shareholders need not be in the country, provided that the company can provide this information promptly on request.

B. Beneficial Ownership Information

7. Countries should follow a multi-pronged approach in order to ensure that the beneficial ownership of a company can be determined in a timely manner by a competent authority. Countries should decide, on the basis of risk, context and materiality, what form of registry or alternative mechanisms they will use to enable efficient access to information by competent authorities, and should document their decision. This should include the following:

a) Countries should require companies to obtain and hold adequate, accurate and up-to-date information on the company's own beneficial ownership; to cooperate with competent authorities to the fullest extent possible in determining the beneficial owner, including making the information available to competent authorities in a timely manner; and to cooperate with financial institutions/DNFBPs to provide adequate, accurate and up-to-date information on the company's beneficial ownership information.

b) (i) Countries should require adequate, accurate and up-to-date information on the beneficial ownership of legal persons to be held by a public

---

[7] The information can be recorded by the company itself or by a third person under the company's responsibility.

[8] This information should be made public, as set out in para 11.

[9] This is applicable to the nominal owner of all registered shares.

[10] Or another public body in the case of a tax identification number.

authority or body (for example a tax authority, FIU, company registry, or beneficial ownership registry). Information need not be held by a single body only.[11]

b) (ii) Countries may decide to use an alternative mechanism instead of (b)(i) if it also provides authorities with efficient access to adequate, accurate and up-to-date BO information. For these purposes reliance on basic information or existing information alone is insufficient, but there must be some specific mechanism that provides efficient access to the information.

c) Countries should use any additional supplementary measures that are necessary to ensure the beneficial ownership of a company can be determined; including for example information held by regulators or stock exchanges; or obtained by financial institutions and/or DNFBPs in accordance with Recommendations 10 and 22.[12]

8. All the persons, authorities and entities mentioned above, and the company itself (or its administrators, liquidators or other persons involved in the dissolution of the company), should maintain the information and records referred to for at least five years after the date on which the company is dissolved or otherwise ceases to exist, or five years after the date on which the company ceases to be a customer of the professional intermediary or the financial institution

C. Timely Access to Adequate, Accurate, and Up-to-Date Information

9. Countries should have mechanisms that ensure that basic information and beneficial ownership information, including information provided to the company registry and any available information referred to in paragraph 7, is adequate, accurate and up to date.

Adequate information is information that is sufficient to identify[13] the natural person(s) who are the beneficial owner(s), and the means and mechanisms through which they exercise beneficial ownership or control.

Accurate information is information, which has been verified to confirm its accuracy by verifying the identity and status of the beneficial owner using reliable, independently sourced/obtained documents, data or information.

---

[11] A body could record beneficial ownership information alongside other information (e.g. basic ownership and incorporation information, tax information), or the source of information could take the form of multiple registries (e.g. for provinces or districts, for sectors, or for specific types of legal person such as NPOs), or of a private body entrusted with this task by the public authority.

[12] Countries should be able to determine in a timely manner whether a company has or controls an account with a financial institution within the country.

[13] Examples of information aimed at identifying the natural person(s) who are the beneficial owner(s) include the full name, nationality(ies), the full date and place of birth, residential address, national identification number and document type, and the tax identification number or equivalent in the country of residence.

The extent of verification measures may vary according to the specific level of risk.

Countries should consider complementary measures as necessary to support the accuracy of beneficial ownership information, e.g. discrepancy reporting.

Up-to-date information is information which is as current and up-to-date as possible, and is updated within a reasonable period (e.g. within one month) following any change.

10. Competent authorities, and in particular law enforcement authorities and FIUs, should have all the powers necessary to be able to obtain timely access to the basic and beneficial ownership information held by the relevant parties, including rapid and efficient access to information held or obtained by a public authority or body or other competent authority on basic and beneficial ownership information, and/or on the financial institutions or DNFBPs which hold this information. In addition, countries should ensure public authorities at national level and others as appropriate have timely access to basic and beneficial ownership information on legal persons in the course of public procurement.

11. Countries should require their company registry to facilitate timely access by financial institutions, DNFBPs and other countries' competent authorities to the public information they hold, and, at a minimum to the information referred to in paragraph 4 (a) above. Countries should also consider facilitating timely access by financial institutions and DNFBPs to information referred to in paragraph 4(b) above and to beneficial ownership information held pursuant to paragraph 7 above, and could consider facilitating public access to this information.

D. Obstacles to Transparency

12. Countries should take measures to prevent and mitigate the risk of the misuse of bearer shares and bearer share warrants[14] by prohibiting the issuance of new bearer shares and bearer share warrants; and, for any existing bearer shares and bearer share warrants, by applying one or more of the following mechanisms within a reasonable timeframe[15]:

    a) converting them into a registered form; or

    b) immobilising them by requiring them to be held with a regulated financial institution or professional intermediary, with timely access to the information by the competent authorities; and

---

[14] Or any other similar instruments without traceability.

[15] These requirements do not apply to newly issued and existing bearer shares or bearer share warrants of a company listed on a stock exchange and subject to disclosure requirements (either by stock exchange rules or through law or enforceable means) which impose requirements to ensure adequate transparency of beneficial ownership.

c) during the period before (a) or (b) is completed, requiring holders of bearer instruments to notify the company, and the company to record their identity before any rights associated therewith can be exercised.

13. Countries should take measures to prevent and mitigate the risk of the misuse of nominee shareholding and nominee directors, by applying one or more of the following mechanisms:

a) requiring nominee shareholders and directors to disclose their nominee status and the identity of their nominator to the company and to any relevant registry, and for this information to be included in the relevant register, and for the information to be obtained, held or recorded by the public authority or body or the alternative mechanism referred to in paragraph 7. Nominee status should be included in public information;

b) requiring nominee shareholders and directors to be licensed[16], for their nominee status and the identity of their nominator to be obtained, held or recorded by the public authority or body or alternative mechanism referred to in paragraph 7 and for them to maintain information identifying their nominator and the natural person on whose behalf the nominee is ultimately acting[17], and make this information available to the competent authorities upon request[18]; or

c) enforcing a prohibition of the use of nominee shareholders or nominee directors.

E. Other Legal Persons

14. In relation to foundations, Anstalt, Waqf[19], and limited liability partnerships, countries should take similar measures and impose similar requirements, as those required for companies, taking into account their different forms and structures.

15. As regards other types of legal persons, countries should take into account the different forms and structures of those other legal persons, and the levels of money laundering and terrorist financing risks associated with each type of legal person, with a view to achieving appropriate levels of transparency. At a minimum, countries should ensure that similar types of basic informa-

---

[16] A country need not impose a separate licensing or registration system with respect to natural or legal persons already licensed or registered as financial institutions or DNFBPs (as defined by the FATF Recommendations) within that country, which, under such license or registration, are permitted to perform nominee activities and which are already subject to the full range of applicable obligations under the FATF Recommendations.

[17] Identifying the beneficial owner in situations where a nominee holds a controlling interest or otherwise exercises effective control requires establishing the identity of the natural person on whose behalf the nominee is ultimately, directly or indirectly, acting.

[18] For intermediaries involved in such nominee activities, reference should be made to R.22 and R.28 in fulfilling the relevant requirements.

[19] Except in countries where Waqf are legal arrangements under R.25.

tion should be recorded and kept accurate and up-to-date by such legal persons, and that such information is accessible in a timely way by competent authorities. Countries should review the money laundering and terrorist financing risks associated with such other legal persons, and, based on the level of risk, determine the measures that should be taken to ensure that competent authorities have timely access to adequate, accurate and up-to-date beneficial ownership information for such legal persons.

F. Liability and Sanctions

16. There should be a clearly stated responsibility to comply with the requirements in this Interpretive Note, as well as liability and effective, proportionate and dissuasive sanctions, as appropriate for any legal or natural person that fails to properly comply with the requirements.

G. International Cooperation

17. Countries should rapidly, constructively and effectively provide the widest possible range of international cooperation in relation to basic and beneficial ownership information, on the basis set out in Recommendations 37 and 40. This should include (a) facilitating access by foreign competent authorities to basic information held by company registries; (b) exchanging information on shareholders; and (c) using their powers, in accordance with their domestic law, to obtain beneficial ownership information on behalf of foreign counterparts. Countries should monitor the quality of assistance they receive from other countries in response to requests for basic and beneficial ownership information or requests for assistance in locating beneficial owners residing abroad. Consistent with Recommendations 37 and 40, countries should not place unduly restrictive conditions on the exchange of information or assistance e.g., refuse a request on the grounds that it involves a fiscal, including tax, matters, bank secrecy, etc. Information held or obtained for the purpose of identifying beneficial ownership should be kept in a readily accessible manner in order to facilitate rapid, constructive and effective international co-operation. Countries should designate and make publicly known the agency(ies) responsible for responding to all international requests for BO information.

PUBLIC STATEMENT ON REVISIONS TO R.24

Paris, 4 March 2022 - The Financial Action Task Force today adopted amendments to Recommendation 24 and its Interpretive Note which require countries to prevent the misuse of legal persons for money laundering or terrorist financing and to ensure that there is adequate, accurate and up-to-date information on the beneficial ownership and control of legal persons.

These amendments represent the outcomes of the two years of work in reviewing the standards. They strengthen the international standards on beneficial ownership of legal persons, to ensure greater transparency about the ultimate ownership and control of legal persons and to mitigate the risks of their misuse. This will significantly strengthen the requirements for beneficial ownership transparency globally, while retaining a degree of flexibility for individual countries to go further in refining individual regimes.

These changes respond to the significant misuse of legal persons for money laundering, terrorist financing, and also for proliferation financing in a number of jurisdictions. FATF Mutual Evaluations show a generally insufficient level of effectiveness in combating the misuse of legal persons for money laundering and terrorist financing globally, and that countries need to do more to implement the current FATF standards promptly, fully and effectively. Both the evolving money laundering risks and the widely publicised failures to prevent misuse of legal persons show that the current standards need to be updated.

These stronger standards are an important first step, but tackling the abuse of legal persons will need constructive and sustained effort by all countries to effectively implement the new standards and respond to risks.

The amendments to Recommendation 24 explicitly require a multi-pronged approach, i.e. to use a combination of different mechanisms, for collection of beneficial ownership information to ensure it is available to competent authorities in a timely manner. Countries should require companies to obtain and hold adequate, accurate and up-to-date information on their own beneficial ownership and make such information available to competent authorities in a timely manner. Countries should also require beneficial ownership information to be held by a public authority or body functioning as beneficial ownership registry or may use an alternative mechanism if such a mechanism also provides efficient access to adequate, accurate and up-to-date beneficial ownership information by competent authorities. Moreover, countries should apply any additional supplementary measures that are necessary to ensure the determination of beneficial ownership of a company. These additional measures include holding beneficial ownership information obtained by regulated financial institutions and professionals, or held by regulators or in stock exchanges.

The revisions to Recommendation 24 will require countries to follow a risk-based approach and consider the risks of legal persons in their countries. They must assess and address the risk posed by legal person, not only by those created in their countries, but also by foreign-created persons which have sufficient links with their country. The changes also specify that access to information by competent authorities should be timely, and information should be adequate for identifying the beneficial owner, accurate - based on verification - and up to date. Furthermore, the revisions require countries to ensure that public authorities have access to beneficial ownership information of legal persons in the course of public procurement. Finally, the changes include stronger controls to prevent the misuse of bearer shares and nominee arrangements, including prohibiting the issuance of new bearer shares and bearer share warrants and conversion or immobilisation of the existing ones, and more robust transparency requirements for nominee arrangements.

In the course of amending Recommendation 24 and its Interpretive Note, the FATF has held two rounds of public consultation to collect stakeholders' views on the key policy areas and proposals. The FATF is thankful for their significant contributions. These contributions indicated strong support for FATF's work to strengthen standards on beneficial ownership and transparency. They also highlighted the need for further Guidance to assist countries and the private sector in meeting these obligations. These responses will inform the FATF's upcoming work to immediately commence the development of comprehensive Guidance to assist countries in implementing the standards.

To facilitate countries' implementation of beneficial ownership registries, the FATF will also analyse the growing practical experience of implementing beneficial ownership registries, with a view to identifying best practices and supporting implementation by countries.

The adopted changes to Recommendation 24 will significantly strengthen the global response to tackling concealment of beneficial ownership of legal persons. The FATF will also begin the process of revising its Methodology for assessing these new obligations. The FATF is, in parallel, reviewing Recommendation 25 on beneficial ownership of legal arrangements, with a view to ensuring consistent where relevant and appropriately tailored beneficial ownership standards and smooth implementation. As part of a phased approach, the FATF will begin assessing jurisdictions for implementation of the revised requirements at the start of the next (fifth) round of mutual evaluations, to allow time to put the necessary domestic measures in place. In the meantime, the FATF will continue to work with the global network to provide the necessary technical assistance and training to help countries meet the prevalent standards, raise awareness of the new obligations, enhance understanding of registries and alternative mechanisms, and improve effectiveness of their implementation.

The FATF expects all countries to take concrete steps to implement these new standards promptly, and to determine the appropriate sequence and timeframe for implementation at national level.

Reproduced from the Financial Action Task Force, https://www.fatf.gafi.org.

Appendix 3. Beneficial Ownership Requirements in Other Aspects of the Financial Action Task Force Standards

The Financial Action Task Force Assessment Methodology

The Financial Action Task Force's (FATF) current assessment methodology includes two separate but linked exercises: an assessment of the country's technical compliance with the standards (that is, the assessment of the country's legal and regulatory framework against the FATF 40 Recommendations), and an assessment of the effectiveness of the country's framework for anti–money laundering and combating the financing of terrorism considering their risks.

Beneficial Ownership Requirements in Other FATF Recommendations

Transparency of beneficial ownership requirements are not isolated in Recommendation 24 but are included in several FATF recommendations, including with respect to Recommendations 25 and 10, as well as other recommendations: 1, 12, 17, 24, 26, 28, and 40. This includes the requirements contained in the interpretive notes to these recommendations. As a result, shortcomings in the implementation of Recommendation 24 and Recommendation 25 can have a negative impact on other recommendations (Appendix Table 3.1).

More specifically, beneficial ownership information transparency is important with respect to all of the following recommendations (highlighted in Appendix Table 3.1):

Understanding risks (Recommendation 1). Recommendation 1 requires that countries assess and understand money laundering and terrorist financing risks and apply a risk-based approach. Although not specifically mentioned in Recommendation 1, an understanding of the money laundering and terrorist financing risks related to legal persons and legal arrangements, including issues related to beneficial ownership transparency, is arguably an important component of understanding money laundering and terrorist financing risks at a national level (and where relevant, a supranational level).

Customer due diligence (CDD) for financial institutions (Recommendation 10), including when relying on third parties (Recommendation 17). As part of their CDD requirements, financial institutions are required to identify and verify beneficial ownership information of their customers who are legal persons. Ideally, they should be able to use information collected by the government (under Recommendation 24) to support their own CDD processes.

Politically exposed persons (Recommendation 12). Reporting entities need to pay particular attention when the beneficial owner of a legal person who is a customer of a financial institution or designated nonfinancial business and profession (DNFBP) that is a legal person is also a politically exposed person, given the higher risks associated with politically exposed persons (such as risk of corruption).

Correspondent banking (Recommendation 13). The FATF guidance on Recommendation 13 notes that when entering and maintaining a business relationship, a correspondent institution should identify and verify the identity of the respondent institution, including to take reasonable measures to verify the identity of the beneficial owner or owners to ensure that the correspondent institution is satisfied that it knows who is the beneficial owner or owners of the respondent institution.

CDD for DNFBP (Recommendation 22). Similar to CDD requirements for legal persons that are a customer of a financial institution, legal persons can also be the customer of a DNFBP. Additionally, some DNFBPs can also have a role in the creation or registration of legal persons and legal arrangements. DNFBPs are therefore required to know the beneficial ownership information of these customers.

Wire transfers (Recommendation 16). Financial institutions are required to undertake CDD when carrying out cross-border wire transfers of more than $1,000 or €1,000, including to identify and take reasonable measures to verify the identity of the beneficial owner of the originator or beneficiary for the wire transfer.

Beneficial owners of financial institutions (Recommendation 26) and beneficial owners of DNFBPs (Recommendation 28). Competent authorities should know who are the beneficial owners of financial institutions and DNFBPs, for example, to prevent criminals from being involved in their ownership or management. If the legal owner is a legal person, then competent authorities must identify the beneficial owner (that is, a natural person) to determine who ultimately owns or controls the financial institution or DNFBP.

International cooperation (Recommendations 36 and 40). Competent authorities must be able to exchange beneficial ownership information with competent authorities in other countries.

APPENDIX TABLE 3.1.

Beneficial Ownership Requirements in FATF Recommendations

R.1 Assessing Risks and Applying a Risk-Based Approach	**R.2** National Cooperation and Coordination	**R.3** Money Laundering Offense	**R.4** Confiscation and Provisional Measures	**R.5** Terrorist Financing Offense	**R.6** Targeted Financial Sanctions Related to Terrorism and Terrorist Financing
R.7 Targeted Financial Sanctions Related to Proliferation	**R.8** Nonprofit Organizations	**R.9** Financial Institution Secrecy Laws	**R.10** Customer Due Diligence	**R.11** Record Keeping	**R.12** Politically Exposed Persons
R.13 Correspondent Banking	**R.14** Money or Value Transfer Services	**R.15** New Technologies	**R.16** Wire Transfers	**R.17** Reliance on Third Parties	**R.18** Internal Controls and Foreign Branches and Subsidiaries
R.19 Higher-Risk Countries	**R.20** Reporting of Suspicious Transactions	**R.21** Tipping Off and Confidentiality	**R.22** DNFBPs: Customer Due Diligence	**R.23** DNFBPs: Other Measures	**R.24** Transparency and Beneficial Ownership of Legal Persons
R.25 Transparency and Beneficial Ownership of Legal Arrangements	**R.26** Regulation and Supervision of Financial Institutions	**R.27** Powers of Supervisors	**R.28** Regulation and Supervision of DNFBPs	**R.29** Financial Intelligence Units	**R.30** Responsibilities of Law Enforcement and Investigative Authorities
R.31 Powers of Law Enforcement and Investigative Authorities	**R.32** Cash Couriers	**R.33** Statistics	**R.34** Guidance and Feedback	**R.35** Sanctions	**R.36** International Instruments
R.37 Mutual Legal Assistance	**R.38** Mutual Legal Assistance: Freezing and Confiscation	**R.39** Extradition	**R.40** Other Forms of International Cooperation		

Sources: Financial Action Task Force; and IMF staff.

Note: DNFBP = designated nonfinancial businesses and professions; FATF = Financial Action Task Force; R. = Recommendation.

Beneficial Ownership Requirements Relevant to the Assessment of Effectiveness

The FATF's assessment of effectiveness is based on 11 immediate outcomes. Each of these links to one or more technical recommendations. For example, the main beneficial ownership Recommendations 24 and 25 link to Immediate Outcome 5 (transparency of legal persons and legal arrangements).

Immediate Outcome 5 assesses the extent to which countries have put effective measures in place to prevent legal persons and arrangements from being used for criminal purposes, make legal persons and arrangements sufficiently transparent, and ensure that accurate and up-to-date basic and beneficial ownership information is available on a timely basis. Basic information should be available publicly, and beneficial ownership information should be available to competent authorities without impediments.

As is the case for technical compliance, lack of effectiveness in the implementation of beneficial ownership requirements can affect immediate outcomes beyond Immediate Outcome 5, and it is relevant (though less directly) to all the other 10 immediate outcomes. The relevant requirements relating to beneficial ownership in the other immediate outcomes are as follows:

- Immediate Outcome 1 (risk, policy and coordination): Countries are required to identify, assess, and understand their money laundering and terrorist financing risks and mitigate them. A comprehensive approach would include any risks relating to transparency of beneficial ownership information.

- Immediate Outcome 2 (international cooperation): Recommendation 24 is specifically mentioned as a relevant recommendation under this immediate outcome. The effectiveness of measures to provide international cooperation in relation to basic and beneficial ownership information will be assessed as one of the core issues.

- Immediate Outcome 3 (supervision): This immediate outcome mentions the concept of beneficial ownership in the context of fitness and propriety of financial institutions and DNFBPs, but it also assesses how supervisors examine compliance with money laundering and terrorist financing measures and the guidance they give on anti–money laundering and combating the financing of terrorism obligations and risks, including beneficial ownership.

- Immediate Outcome 4 (CDD and preventive measures): The CDD measures applied by financial institutions and DNFBPs relating to, inter alia, beneficial ownership are among the effectiveness measures assessed in this immediate outcome.

- Immediate Outcome 6 (use of financial intelligence): The "other relevant information" used by competent authorities includes company registry information and CDD information obtained by financial institutions and DNFBPs. This would include beneficial ownership information.

- Immediate Outcome 7 (money laundering investigation and prosecution): Competent authorities may need to trace beneficial ownership information in the context of a money laundering investigation, and not having timely access to this information can have an impact on their effectiveness in carrying out these investigations.

- Immediate Outcome 8 (confiscation of assets relating to money laundering): The ability to trace beneficial ownership information during the pursuit of assets related to money laundering is a consideration when assessing effectiveness under this immediate outcome.

- Immediate Outcome 9 (terrorist financing investigations): The ability to trace the beneficial ownership of a legal person could be relevant to terrorist financing investigations, especially if the legal person or its beneficial owner has links to terrorist financing activities.

- Immediate Outcome 10 (targeted financial sanctions related to terrorist financing): Tracing designated persons or entities who might be beneficial owners of legal persons is relevant to this immediate outcome.

- Immediate Outcome 11 (targeted financial sanctions related to proliferation financing): Tracing proliferation financing designated persons or entities, and especially how well financial institutions and DNFBPs are implementing proliferation financing requirements that involve legal persons and their beneficial owners, is relevant to Immediate Outcome 11.

Appendix 4. Useful Resources

International Standards on Combating Money Laundering and the Financing of Terrorism & Proliferation: The FATF Recommendations, by the Financial Action Task Force (2022, Financial Action Task Force). https://www.fatf-gafi.org/media/fatf /documents/recommendations/pdfs/FATF%20Recommendations%202012.pdf.

Public Statement on Revisions to Recommendation 24, by the Financial Action Task Force (2022, Financial Action Task Force). https://www.fatf-gafi.org/publications /fatfrecommendations/documents/r24-statement-march-2022.html.

The following resources came into place before the FATF standards were revised, and therefore do not capture or reflect the March 2022 FATF standard on beneficial ownership. However, they can be useful with respect to some of the key issues.

A Beneficial Ownership Implementation Toolkit, by the Global Forum on Transparency and Exchange of Information for Tax Purposes and Inter-American Development Bank. (2019, Inter-American Development Bank and Organisation for Economic Co-operation and Development). https://publications.iadb.org/en/beneficial -ownership-implementation-toolkit.

Best Practices on Beneficial Ownership for Legal Persons, by the Financial Action Task Force. (2019, Financial Action Task Force). https://www.fatf-gafi.org/media /fatf/documents/Best-Practices-Beneficial-Ownership-Legal-Persons.pdf.

Building Effective Beneficial Ownership Frameworks: A Joint Global Forum and Inter-Amercian Development Bank Toolkit. (2022, Inter-American Development Bank and Organisation for Economic Co-operation and Development). https:// www.oecd.org/tax/transparency/documents/effective-beneficial-ownership -frameworks-toolkit_en.pdf.

Concealment of Beneficial Ownership, by the Financial Action Task Force and Egmont Group of Financial Intelligence Units. (2018, Financial Action Task Force and Egmont Group). https://www.fatf-gafi.org/media/fatf/documents /reports/FATF-Egmont-Concealment-beneficial-ownership.pdf.

Guidance on Transparency and Beneficial Ownership, by the Financial Action Task Force. (2014, Financial Action Task Force). https://www.fatf-gafi.org/media/fatf /documents/reports/Guidance-transparency-beneficial-ownership.pdf.

Puppet Masters: How the Corrupt Use Legal Structures to Hide Stolen Assets and What to Do about It, by Emile van der Does de Willebois, Emily M. Halter, Robert A. Harrison, Ji Won Park, and J. C. Sharman. (2011, World Bank). https://openknowledge.worldbank.org/bitstream/handle/10986/2363 /9780821388945.pdf?sequence=6&isAllowed=y.

Signature for Sales: How Nominee Services for Shell Companies Are Abused to Conceal Beneficial Owners, by Daniel Neilson and Jason Sharman. (2022, World Bank). https://star.worldbank.org/publications/signatures-sale-how-nominee-services-shell-companies-are-abused-conceal-beneficial.

Stolen Asset Recovery Country Beneficial Ownership Guides, by the World Bank and the United Nations Office on Drugs and Crime. (World Bank). https://star.worldbank.org/resources.

Select Examples of Beneficial Ownership Registries

Appendix Table 4.1 provides examples of beneficial ownership registries or related mechanisms that hold beneficial ownership information. This information is accurate as of February 2022. We do not hold any views on the effectiveness of these mechanisms/registries, which will be determined case by case in the context of mutual evaluations. The objective here is to provide examples of the types of systems currently in place.

APPENDIX TABLE 4.1.

Examples of Beneficial Ownership Registries as of February 2022

Country	Entity Responsible	Key Features
Austria	Federal Ministry of Finance	Public (payment of fees required); centralized register, operational since 2018; information collected from legal persons
		Data must be checked by the legal entity at least once a year to determine whether the beneficial owners reported to the register are still up to date.
Belgium	Federal Public Service Finance	Public (payment of fees required); centralized register, operational since 2018
Bulgaria	Registry Agency, Ministry of Justice	Public; centralized register, operational since 2019
		All legal entities must be registered.
Canada	Corporations Canada	Public (free)
		The website specifically mentions that corporate, directors, and historical information is public.
Denmark	Danish Business Authority	Public (free for viewing documents, fees for purchasing hard copies); centralized
		Virtually every Danish company must be included.
France	French National Institute of Industrial Property	Public (free); centralized, operational since 2017 and publicly available since 2021
Ghana	Registrar-General's Department	Public (free); centralized
Hong Kong SAR	Financial Services and the Treasury Bureau	Public (identification required)
Indonesia	Ministry of Law and Human Rights	Public (fees required); centralized
Israel	Israeli Corporations Authority, Ministry of Justice	Public (fees required for shareholder information)
		Israeli lawyers submit the vast majority of all registered company applications.
Jersey	Financial Services Commission	Nonpublic for information related to ultimate beneficial ownership; centralized register, operational since 2021

(continued)

APPENDIX TABLE 4.1. CONTINUED

Country	Entity Responsible	Key Features
Kenya	Business Registration Service, Office of the Attorney General and Department of Justice	Public (registration required); centralized
Latvia	Latvia Register of Enterprises	Public (free); centralized register
Luxembourg	Luxembourg Business Registers	Public (free); centralized register, searchable by name of company or business register number
Nigeria	Nigeria Extractive Industries Transparency Initiative	Public (free); sector specific (extractive industries)
Poland	Minister of Public Finance	Public (free); centralized register, operational since 2019
Slovak Republic	Statistical Office of the Slovak Republic	Public (free); centralized register Second industry-specific beneficial ownership register requires any company wanting to compete for government contracts to register on the Register of Public Sector Partners, supervised by the Ministry of Justice.
Slovenia	Agency of the Republic of Slovenia for Public Legal Records and Related Services	Public; registration required to access full information
United Kingdom	Companies House	Public; centralized register, operational since 2016

Index